# THE ULTIMATE HOLLYWOOD TRIVIA QUIZ

**OTHER BOOKS IN THIS SERIES**
*San Francisco Trivia*

# THE ULTIMATE HOLLYWOOD TRIVIA QUIZ

Karen Warner & Michael Iapoce

101 Productions
San Francisco

Cover Design and Illustration: John Allen Hull
Text Photographs: Bruce Torrence Historical Collection
Text Design: Lynne O'Neil

Cover illustration copyright 1986 by John Allen Hull.

Many film reference books give conflicting dates for film releases. The source used for release dates in *The Ultimate Hollywood Trivia Quiz* is *Halliwell's Filmgoer's Companion,* 8th Edition, by Leslie Halliwell. New York: Charles Scribner's Sons, 1985.

Copyright ©1986 Karen Warner and Michael Iapoce.
Printed in the United States of America.
All rights reserved. No part of this book may be reproduced in any form without the written permission of the publisher.

Published by 101 Productions, 834 Mission Street, San Francisco, California 94103
Distributed to the book trade in the United States by The Macmillan Publishing Company, New York.

**Library of Congress Cataloging-in-Publication Data**

Warner, Karen.
  The ultimate Hollywood trivia quiz.

  Includes index.
  1. Moving-pictures—United States—Miscellanea.
2. Hollywood (Los Angeles, Calif.)—Miscellanea.
I. Iapoce, Michael. II. Title.
PN1993.85W28   1986      791.43'02     86-2428
ISBN 0-89286-263-7

TO MOO MOO AND JO JO.———K.W.
FOR MY FATHER WHO TAUGHT ME TO LOVE THE LATE SHOW———M.I.

# CONTENTS

**Only in Hollywood 1**
**A Remarkable History 35**
**Behind the Scenes 69**
**Legends 103**
**A Town Called Hollywood 137**
**There's No Business Like 171**

# Only in Hollywood

# ROMANTIC SHENANIGANS
## Kiss and Tell

1. When asked what caused the breakup of her marriage to actor Ronald Reagan, what reason did Jane Wyman give?

2. In December 1953 Zsa Zsa Gabor sported an eye patch to conceal a shiner allegedly given her by Porfirio Rubirosa. What did she say prompted the swing?

3. John F. Kennedy is rumored to have used the bungalows of this celebrity hotel for an occasional discreet tête-à-tête.

4. Vivien Leigh was said to be put off by her co-star's denture breath and refused to continue filming the love scenes until the problem was remedied. Who was her "foul-mouthed" acting partner?

5. In order to ensure that Glenn Ford and Rita Hayworth were not fooling around during breaks on the set of *Gilda* (1946), studio head Harry Cohn resorted to what extreme tactic?

6. When Lita Grey divorced this movie comedian in 1927, copies of the bill of divorcement sold on the newsstands for a quarter.

7. According to James Bacon, when this Hollywood couple was living in Maine the actor in question, while under the influence of alcohol, shoved his famous actress wife out of their car and into a snow drift. Who was the battling duo?

8. Who was Bella Darvi?

9. When he was arrested for drunken driving, actor John Agar told a courtroom his alcohol problems were caused by his unhappy first marriage. Name the actress who was blamed for John's misfortune.

10. According to biographer Albert Goldman, Elvis Presley was turned on by teenage girls who wore a particular article of clothing. What was Elvis's fantasy dress code?

ANSWERS

# ROMANTIC SHENANIGANS
## Kiss and Tell

1   She said, "He talked too much."

2   Her turning down his marriage proposal. The millionaire denied hitting Ms. Gabor and on New Year's Eve he married Barbara Hutton.

3   The Beverly Hills Hotel.

4   Clark Gable.

5   Cohn had Hayworth's dressing room bugged.

6   Charles Chaplin. The bill contained such tidbits as accusing Chaplin of spying on her, asking her to have an abortion, and reading her pornographic material.

7   Gary Merrill and Bette Davis.

8   The nontalented star of *The Egyptian* (1954), she was Darryl F. Zanuck's paramour. After ingratiating herself to both Virginia and Darryl, she was invited to live in the couple's guesthouse by the unsuspecting Mrs. Zanuck. Both Bella and Darryl found their suitcases on the sidewalk when their amorous adventures were discovered.

9   Shirley Temple. When they divorced, Agar was charged with wife beating.

10  Presley wanted his women to wear white cotton panties.

ONLY IN HOLLYWOOD

# GOOD GUYS (AND GALS)

1. As a teenager, this future actress embroidered her sweaters with the initials *NN* for "non-necker."

2. Marlon Brando cast her in *The Ugly American* in 1962 to help her break her blacklist taboo.

3. When this actor-singer-songwriter died in December 1973, his body was donated to the UCLA Medical Research Department.

4. Warner Oland, best known for his role as good guy Charlie Chan, also played in the first of a series of films about a diabolic Chinese bad guy. Who?

5. Name the cowboy of the silver screen who was noted for wearing his white suit and cowboy boots to even the most fashionable of Hollywood parties.

6. How did Elizabeth Taylor save Montgomery Clift's life?

7. Olivia de Havilland borrowed something from Roy Rogers to use in the making of the 1938 film *The Adventures of Robin Hood*. What did she borrow?

8. While filming *Beau Geste* on location near Yuma, Arizona, actor Gary Cooper got word that his daughter was ill. What unusual means of transportation did he use to get to a telephone?

9. Name the baseball great that coached Gary Cooper in the fine art of baseball for his role as Lou Gehrig in *Pride of the Yankees* (1942).

10. A seaman from Spain, he was "discovered" when his ship was being repaired at Baltimore in 1921.

ANSWERS

# GOOD GUYS (AND GALS)

1   Debbie Reynolds. You were expecting maybe Marilyn Monroe?

2   His actress sister Jocelyn Brando. She reputedly had communist leanings and was blacklisted from Hollywood in the 1950s.

3   Bobby Darin died at age thirty-seven. He had received an Academy Award nomination for his performance in *Captain Newman, M.D.* (1963).

4   Fu Manchu, in *The Mysterious Dr. Fu Manchu* (1929). Fu, as his friends called him, was also played by Boris Karloff, in *The Mask of Fu Manchu* (1932).

5   Tom Mix. Prior to his becoming a movie cowboy, Mix had been a soldier of fortune and had fought in the Spanish-American War, the Boxer Rebellion, and the Boer War.

6   In May 1956 Clift's car hit a tree after he left a dinner party at Taylor's house. Liz reached down Clift's throat and removed the two front teeth that were blocking his windpipe.

7   His horse, Trigger.

8   Cooper rode the almost twenty miles to the nearest phone on a camel.

9   Lefty O'Doul. Gehrig was a southpaw, and since actor Cooper was right-handed, the movie was flopped so Cooper would appear to be a lefty.

10  Duncan Renaldo, known to millions as the Cisco Kid, got his break from a movie director who hired him to draw sketches of the Havana docks for a movie set.

ONLY IN HOLLYWOOD

# NOT ALL AWARDS ARE OSCARS

1. The man claiming to be the only director to make two pictures with Marilyn Monroe said of his accomplishment: "It behooves the Screen Directors Guild to award me a Purple Heart." Who was he?

2. Adolphe Menjou, always a suave and debonair movie villain, was perennially honored outside Hollywood with what distinction?

3. This film represented the only instance when a Nobel prize–winning author was adapted for the screen by *another* Nobel prize–winning author.

4. In 1940 Bette Davis was named queen of the movies by columnist Ed Sullivan. Who was named king that year?

5. Only one movie star has made the list of Top Ten Box Office Draws every year since 1968 (through 1985, the time of this writing). Who?

6. In 1971 the Marine Corps League named him "The man who best exemplifies the word American."

7. The *Harvard Lampoon* gave Jane Fonda this distinction for her performance in the 1962 film *The Chapman Report*.

8. In 1926 Will Rogers was named First Honorary Mayor of Beverly Hills. What did he say was his chief official duty?

9. In January 1986 Katharine Hepburn said when being honored with this award, "We're in a serious spot here when the original bag lady ends up inspiring dressing." Why was she being recognized?

10. While living a hippie life style in the 1960s, Michael Douglas's parents demanded he support himself. The resourceful future actor-producer got himself a job in the oil industry. What was it?

ANSWERS

# NOT ALL AWARDS ARE OSCARS

1  Billy Wilder. He directed her in *The Seven Year Itch* (1955) and again in *Some Like It Hot* (1959). Marilyn had made two pictures with others (e.g., Hawks's 1953 *Gentlemen Prefer Blondes* and 1952 *Monkey Business*), but Wilder had her at her most unmanageable.

2  Menjou was regularly included on the list of the world's Ten Best-Dressed Men.

3  *To Have and Have Not* (1945). The screenplay from Ernest Hemingway's novel was written by William Faulkner (along with Jules Furthman).

4  Mickey Rooney. According to Davis, Rooney would not wear his crown during the award ceremonies.

5  Clint Eastwood.

6  John Wayne.

7  She was named Worst Actress of the Year.

8  Directing people to Pickfair, the famous home of Mary Pickford and Douglas Fairbanks.

9  She had just won a lifetime achievement award from the Council of Fashion Designers of America.

10  Michael supported himself working in a gas station and distinguished himself by becoming Mobil Man of the Month.

ONLY IN HOLLYWOOD

# MMM . . . THAT'S GOOD!
## Food and Other Good Things to Eat

1. As a young actor, Brando's favorite breakfast consisted of:
   a) A two-pound T-bone steak.   b) A raw egg and orange juice.
   c) Wheat germ and carrot sticks.

2. The production of the 1925 silent epic *Quo Vadis?*, a film about Emperor Nero, was marred by an unfortunate accident involving one of the animals on the set. What happened?

3. William Randolph Hearst was famous for throwing lavish parties at his San Simeon estate. He did have a peculiar request when it came to linen for the table, however. He insisted upon using paper napkins. Why?

4. His store, The Posh Bagel, opened in Beverly Hills in 1975.

5. Name the actress who is best known for having James Cagney push a grapefruit in her face in the film *Public Enemy* (1931).

6. Who is credited with starting the pie-throwing craze of the Keystone Kops movies?

7. Name the film that inspired a Quaker Oats candy bar to be created in its honor.

8. Designer John Truscott decorated the bridal dress in this 1967 film, that was adapted from the stage play, with tiny seashells and pumpkin seeds.

9. In the 1985 horror film *Day of the Dead*, zombies feast on a bad guy, tearing him limb from limb. But they are not really nibbling on his kneecaps. What are they eating?

10. Name the Woody Allen movie in which the Japanese hero, Phil Moskowitz, is tracking down a stolen recipe for egg salad.

ANSWERS

# MMM . . . THAT'S GOOD!
# Food and Other Good Things to Eat

1   A raw egg and orange juice.

2   A lion, kept hungry so as to act more ferocious, got loose and ate one of the extras.

3   WRH thought it was more sanitary.

4   Burt Reynolds.

5   Mae Clark, who claims the grapefruit scene was done for a laugh and was amazed that it was included in the film.

6   Mabel Normand. During a break at the studio, Mabel went to a bakery and bought herself a pie. When she returned one of the crew members teased her about the pie. Just as Mack Sennett was coming in the door, Mabel flung the pie in her assailant's face. The rest is film history.

7   *Willy Wonka and the Chocolate Factory* (1971). Quaker Oats manufactured the Willy Wonka Super Skrunch Bar. The candy bar suffered from the same fate as the film: kids stayed away from it in droves.

8   *Camelot*. The dress was worn by Vanessa Redgrave and the film garnered Truscott an Academy Award.

9   Turkey legs barbecued in a special sauce to look like human flesh . . . yuck!

10  *What's Up, Tiger Lily?* (1966).

ONLY IN HOLLYWOOD

# TALK ABOUT BAD LUCK

1. The three principal characters in *Rebel Without a Cause* (1955) were all to meet with untimely real-life deaths. Who were they?

2. Recent revelations indicate that this dashing adventure hero may have been guilty of treason during World War II.

3. This British-born actor received his only Academy Award posthumously, dying some two months before the ceremony.

4. In 1952 Humphrey Bogart won the Best Actor Oscar for his performance in *The African Queen*. Brando was favored to win the Academy Award that year for which movie?

5. This bad guy made a career of turning down tough-guy roles that would eventually go to Humphrey Bogart.

6. Through a bizarre set of circumstances, bit actor Bill Meade was impaled on his own sword after being thrown from his horse during the filming of this cavalry-and-Indian movie.

7. This Hollywood actor died in the New York apartment of former actress Iris Whitney in 1952.

8. When movie director William Desmond Taylor was found shot to death in the unsolved murder of February 1, 1922, two actresses were soon discovered to be his lovers and their careers promptly ended. Who were the actresses?

9. At age twenty, he made a fortune in Hollywood building sound stages for the "new" talking movies.

10. Name the actor whose face was used as a model for Satan's in the Walt Disney production *Fantasia* (1940).

ANSWERS

# TALK ABOUT BAD LUCK

1. James Dean (car crash), Natalie Wood (drowned), and Sal Mineo (stabbed to death).

2. Errol Flynn, in addition to his wicked romantic ways, is now alleged to have worked secretly for the Nazis.

3. Peter Finch was not around to collect his Best Actor Oscar for *Network* (1976).

4. *A Streetcar Named Desire*. Brando starred as Stanley Kowalski and some thought he lost the Oscar because of his contempt for Hollywood.

5. George Raft, for various reasons, turned down leads in *Casablanca* (1942), *The Maltese Falcon* (1941), *High Sierra* (1941), and *Dead End* (1937).

6. *They Died with Their Boots On* (1941).

7. John Garfield, star of such films as *Tortilla Flat* (1942) and *The Postman Always Rings Twice* (1946), was married at the time of his death to his wife of almost two decades, Robbie.

8. Mabel Normand and Mary Miles Minter. The amorous Taylor had abandoned a wife and child in New York and was carrying on love affairs with the two actresses at the same time.

9. Mike Todd, who went broke when the Great Depression hit.

10. Bela Lugosi.

ONLY IN HOLLYWOOD

# HOLLYWOOD ROCKS AND ROLLS

1. Name the 1956 film featuring Bill Haley and the Comets that prompted worldwide controversy, including the comment from Egypt calling it an American plot "designed to sow trouble in the Middle East by undermining Egyptian morale."

2. Name the co-star of the 1959 teenage surfing movie *Gidget* who started his own surfboard company.

3. Name the actor who portrayed these characters on the silver screen: Tulsa McLean, Lucky Jackson, Joe Lightcloud, and Dr. John Carpenter.

4. Name the rock-and-roll classic that opened the film *The Blackboard Jungle* (1955).

5. She was the singing voice of Tuesday Weld in *Rock, Rock, Rock* (1956).

6. Name the two unlikely stars of the 1956 rock-and-roll film that features such rock greats as Little Richard, Eddie Cochran, Fats Domino, and The Platters.

7. The opening scene of this rock film is of Jerry Lee Lewis rocking out on a piano, which is perched on a moving flatbed truck.

8. The 1958 movie *High School Confidential!* featured which of these famous Hollywood offspring?
    a) Charles Chaplin, Jr.   b) John Barrymore, Jr.   c) William Wellman, Jr.

9. The 1964 rock production *Get Yourself a College Girl* featured a lovely co-ed who was in real life a former Miss America. Who was she?

10. Name the rock movie that marked the only screen appearance of Richie Valens.

ANSWERS
# HOLLYWOOD ROCKS AND ROLLS

1  *Rock Around the Clock.*

2  Taking his inspiration from the movie, The Cliff Robertson Surf Board Company, in Venice, California, was the first of its kind on the West Coast.

3  Elvis Presley played these memorable parts in *G.I. Blues* (1960), *Viva Las Vegas* (1964), *Stay Away Joe* (1968), and *Change of Habit* (1969), respectively.

4  "Rock Around the Clock" by Bill Haley and the Comets. When the song was first released in 1954 it met with little success. The movie sent the record to the top of the charts.

5  Connie Francis. Connie did her own singing in the rock movies *Where the Boys Are* (1960), *Follow the Boys* (1963), and *Looking for Love* (1964).

6  Tom Ewell and Jayne Mansfield in *The Girl Can't Help It.*

7  *High School Confidential!* (1958).

8  All of them.

9  Mary Ann Mobley.

10  *Go, Johnny, Go* (1958). In the film Valens sang his famous "La Bamba." Shortly after he completed the movie he was killed in a plane crash.

ONLY IN HOLLYWOOD

# HEY YOU!
## Nicknames

1. Who called one-time husband Douglas Fairbanks, Jr. "Dodo" and referred to Spencer Tracy as "Slug"?

2. This former model was known as The Windmill and Pinwheel.

3. Sometimes known as Frantic Frog because of her busy schedule at the studio, she was also called Fretting Frog by crew members who had to deal with her on-set demands.

4. She was called Peaches by the boys while growing up in Brooklyn, New York.

5. During the filming of *Gone With the Wind*, director Victor Fleming's name for Vivien Leigh was from a familiar line of her dialogue. What did he call her?

6. Mary Pickford was known as America's Sweetheart. How did she get the nickname?

7. How did Clark Gable come to be known as The King?

8. According to Sheilah Graham, what was Richard Burton's nickname for Liz Taylor?
    a) Fatty.   b) Beloved.   c) Tons of Fun.   d) My Pet.

9. How did John Wayne get the nickname Duke?

10. Why is the Academy Award known as the Oscar?

ANSWERS

# HEY YOU!
# Nicknames

1   Hollywood's meanest mama, Joan Crawford.

2   Lauren Bacall, because of her long arms and legs.

3   Claudette Colbert.

4   Mae West.

5   Fiddle-dee-dee.

6   During World War I, Mary and Sid Grauman were in San Francisco for a parade of the Third Field Artillery. Mary was made an honorary army colonel and the crowd was cheering the troops and Mary. Reportedly Sid turned to Pickford and said "America is a wonderful country and you're America's sweetheart."

7   Syndicated columnist Ed Sullivan had a contest in 1937 in which his 20 million readers voted on the king and queen of Hollywood. Gable was selected as king and Myrna Loy as queen.

8   Fatty.

9   As a child he had a dog named Duke who liked to romp around firehouses. The firefighters dubbed the pair Big Duke and Little Duke. Wayne, incidentally, was the latter.

10  Legend has it that Bette Davis named her Academy Award for her first husband, Ham Oscar Nelson, because the statuette's fanny resembled her husband's. She won the Oscar for *Dangerous* (1935).

## SEX SYMBOLS
## Some Like It Hotter

1. He has the distinction of giving a grown-up Shirley Temple her first kiss in the movie *Kiss and Tell* (1945).

2. Which of the following were sequels to Clint Eastwood's *Dirty Harry* (1971)?
   a) *Magnum Force* (1973).   b) *The Enforcer* (1976).
   c) *The Gauntlet* (1977).   d) *Tightrope* (1984).
   e) *Hog's Breath Inn* (1974).

3. Jeanette MacDonald gave up her own salary for this movie in order to lure this actor as her co-star. Name the actor and the movie.

4. In the 1957 British film *Sea Wife*, this sex bomb plays the unlikely role of a Catholic nun.

5. In his film debut, he dies toward the end of the movie, a Civil War melodrama originally titled *The Reno Brothers*.

6. Gloria Swanson played a silent version of this Somerset Maugham character in 1928. Joan Crawford and Rita Hayworth played the talking versions in 1932 and 1953, respectively. Who was the sexy character played by the three actresses?

7. At his request Annette Funicello did not bare her navel in any of her "beach" movies.

8. His 1930s bachelor pad in Beverly Hills was decorated with trophies he had collected while on an African safari.

9. Name the German-born actress star of *Hotel Imperial* (1927), who in a 1936 interview claimed to have had a romantic interlude with Hitler.

10. Name the actor who has been described as a Lush Lothario, Technicolor Tarzan, and an Overripe Romeo.

ANSWERS

# SEX SYMBOLS
## Some Like It Hotter

1   Jerome Courtland.

2   *Magnum Force* and *The Enforcer*. Eastwood played different cops in *The Gauntlet* and *Tightrope*. Hog's Breath Inn is the name of his restaurant in Carmel, California.

3   Clark Gable in *San Francisco* (1936). Gable was at first reluctant to play opposite the scene-stealing soprano.

4   Joan Collins.

5   Elvis Presley in *Love Me Tender* (1956). The movie was renamed after one of the love ballads Presley sings in the film.

6   Sadie Thompson, which was also the title of the 1928 version. The 1932 film was called *Rain*, and the 1953 version was *Miss Sadie Thompson*.

7   Walt Disney asked the ex-Mouseketeer to keep her belly button under wraps.

8   Gary Cooper. In addition to zebra-skin rugs and mounted lion heads, Coop had a pet chimpanzee as a reminder of his trip to Africa.

9   Pola Negri.

10  Victor Mature.

ONLY IN HOLLYWOOD

# THE BOOB TUBE
## Hollywood Watches Television

1. According to a *TV Guide* poll, this movie is shown on television more frequently than any other, no doubt making it the "most-viewed" movie of all time.

2. Sheilah Graham broke into television in the late 1940s doing a commentary and an interview at what occasion?

3. After Universal Studios declined to pick up his option in 1952, he did a TV series and some European films before becoming the biggest box-office draw in Hollywood history.

4. Character actor Chill Wills played a major behind-the-scenes role in a series of movies about a well-known animal. Name his role and the animal.

5. This popular 1955 Walt Disney adventure was created by editing three one-hour episodes from his TV show into a feature film.

6. *Rocky III* first introduced America to one of its most successful pop culture heroes of the 1980s. Who?

7. *The First Nudie Musical* (1976), a spoof of both porno and musical movies, features this unlikely female star from a hit television series.

8. In 1959 Charles Collingwood's "Person to Person" interview with this star was left on the cutting room floor when CBS censors determined it too suggestive.

9. Millionaire Lynn Atkinson built an extravagant mansion in Bel Air in 1935 as a surprise for his wife. What became of the house in later years?

10. Name the twenty-one year old who in 1969 directed Joan Crawford in her first television movie for the then-new "Night Gallery."

ANSWERS

# THE BOOB TUBE
## Hollywood Watches Television

1   *Casablanca* (1942).

2   She interviewed pro wrestler Gorgeous George, after doing the commentary on one of his matches. Could Rona Barrett have done that?

3   Clint Eastwood starred in TV's "Rawhide" and several spaghetti westerns before becoming a major star.

4   He was the voice of Francis the Talking Mule, as well as of TV's Mr. Ed.

5   *Davy Crockett, King of the Wild Frontier*. Disney was taken by surprise by the sensation Davy created through the TV episodes, and the movie quickly took advantage of this phenomenon. The following year, two new TV episodes were put together and released as *Davy Crockett and the River Pirates*.

6   Mr. T starred as Rocky's nemesis, Clubber Lang, in the 1982 sequel to a sequel, and went on to fame and fortune in TV's "A-Team."

7   Cindy Williams, star of TV's "Laverne and Shirley." The movie was given an R rating.

8   Mae West, who had a problem with censors her entire professional career.

9   The house was used on the TV show "The Beverly Hillbillies." Atkinson got a big surprise when his wife saw the flamboyant estate. She said it was pretentious and they never moved into the house.

10  Steven Spielberg, who at the time was a rookie at Universal Studios.

ONLY IN HOLLYWOOD

# CHILDREN IN THE MOVIES
## Go Away, Kid, You Bother Me

1. This eight year old was discovered almost simultaneously by two studios, after being noticed in two different places: at her dancing class and her mother's art gallery.

2. What happened when Jackie Coogan turned twenty-one and asked his mother for the fortune he had earned as a child actor?

3. Name the child actor who won a special Oscar for his role in *The Yearling* (1946).

4. In his autobiography this former child star claimed to have had an affair with Joan Crawford.

5. This child star was discovered at age three modeling for a cover of *Saturday Evening Post*.

6. Name the child star that replaced Farina in the Our Gang comedy films.

7. In *The Proud Rebel* (1956), this child actor co-starred with his father, who played the role of a mute. Who was the father-and-son acting team?

8. Name the Brooke Shields movie that was banned in England.

9. When Louis B. Mayer told child actress Margaret O'Brien she could have anything she wanted for her birthday, what did she ask for?

10. A picture of this teenage movie star was found on the wall above Anne Frank's bed in her family's hidden living quarters in Nazi-occupied Amsterdam.

ANSWERS

# CHILDREN IN THE MOVIES
## Go Away, Kid, You Bother Me

1   Little Elizabeth Taylor made a screen test for both MGM and Universal, signing her first contract with the latter.

2   His mother, citing a California law that states the earnings of a minor are the property of the parents, refused to share any of the estimated $4 million Coogan had earned as a child star.

3   Claude Jarman, Jr. He now lives in San Francisco and works for a large company in corporate communications.

4   Jackie Cooper claims that as a teenager he had numerous romantic encounters with the very adult Joan Crawford.

5   Larry Simms was spotted on the cover of the magazine and signed for the part of Baby Dumpling in the Blondie film series.

6   "Stymie" Matthew Beard, who made his film debut at age one and a half in *Uncle Tom's Cabin* (1927).

7   Alan and David Ladd. In 1973 David married Cheryl Jean Stoppelmoor, who as Cheryl Ladd was a hit on the TV series "Charlie's Angels."

8   *Pretty Baby* (1978). In the film the prepubescent Shields plays a child prostitute in 1917 New Orleans.

9   Lassie.

10  Deanna Durbin.

ONLY IN HOLLYWOOD

# IT'S A FAMILY AFFAIR
## Everything Is Relative

1. This father and son picked up a total of four Oscars for their work in a 1975 hit film.

2. One member of Alfred Hitchcock's family appears in his *Stage Fright* (1950), *Strangers on a Train* (1951), and *Psycho* (1960). Who?

3. When little Liza Minnelli lived at her father Vincente's Beverly Hills home in the early 1950s (six months a year per divorce agreement with Judy Garland), she kept a rather unique set of "playclothes" in her closet. What were they?

4. Three brothers named Leonard, Adolph, and Julius created one of Hollywood's greatest "family" teams, starring in films from the late twenties to the early fifties. Who were they?

5. MGM put this star's mother in charge of its talent school, partly to keep her off the set of her daughter's pictures.

6. As a child he was paid $2.50 an hour to read scripts with his father to help him memorize his lines. Name the famous father and son.

7. When she wrote this classic Hollywood exposé, she claimed it was to call attention to the issue of child abuse.

8. Name the granddaughter of architect Frank Lloyd Wright who won an Oscar for Best Supporting Actress in *The Razor's Edge* (1946).

9. Who played the part of the infant Moses in the 1956 version of the film *The Ten Commandments*?

10. Director Peter Bogdanovich said of the 1973 film *Paper Moon*: "One of the most miserable experiences of my life." Name the novice actress that caused the director so much distress.

ANSWERS

# IT'S A FAMILY AFFAIR
## Everything Is Relative

1. Carmine Coppola won an Academy Award for Original Musical Score and son Francis Ford Coppola won three more Oscars for *The Godfather, Part II*.

2. His daughter Patricia.

3. Dad provided her with costumes, in her own size, from famous movies. Friends like Candice Bergen sometimes came over to play *Gone With the Wind*!

4. Better known as Chico, Harpo, and Groucho, they were the Marx Brothers.

5. Lela Rogers, Ginger's mother, had been a Marine sergeant in World War I and was still quite formidable.

6. Peter and Henry Fonda.

7. Christina Crawford's *Mommie Dearest* revealed the dark side of her adoptive mother, Joan Crawford.

8. Anne Baxter, whose most memorable role was as Eve Harrington in *All About Eve* (1950).

9. Charlton Heston's three-month-old son Fraser.

10. Tatum O'Neal, who starred with her father Ryan in the movie and managed to capture an Oscar for her efforts.

# WHO WAS THAT?
## The Good, the Bad, and the Ugly

1  In 1935 the *New York Times Magazine* described this star as "the best known and most popular international figure of his day." Who was he?

2  The Three Stooges consisted of Moe Howard, Larry Fine, and a series of four other men who played the third "stooge." Who were they?

3  Name the actress who turned down the part of Blanche du Bois in *A Streetcar Named Desire* (1951) because she considered the role unladylike.

4  According to actress Terry Moore, Howard Hughes loved only three women in his life. Name them.

5  Victor McLaglen, a silent-movie bad guy and later Oscar winner for his role as *The Informer* (1935), once boxed a heavyweight champion. Who?

6  Match the western "kid" and the movie in which he appears:
    The Ringo Kid.                 *Blazing Saddles* (1974).
    The Abilene Kid.               *Cat Ballou* (1965).
    Kid Shelleen.                  *Three Godfathers* (1948).
    The Waco Kid.                 *Stagecoach* (1939).

7  In order to persuade this actor to play Sergeant York, Jesse L. Lasky sent a telegram to him and signed the message Sgt. Alvin C. York.

8  He chose his acting name because he admired Douglas Fairbanks.

9  In the 1946 version of *Humoresque*, who played the violin for star John Garfield?

10  Martin Kosleck portrayed this World War II Nazi in four Hollywood films.

ANSWERS

# WHO WAS THAT?
## The Good, the Bad, and the Ugly

1   Mickey Mouse.

2   Curly Howard, Shemp Howard, Joe Besser, and Joe DeRita. In all, The Three Stooges appeared in twenty-three feature films and close to two hundred shorts.

3   Olivia de Havilland. She was replaced by Vivien Leigh who garnered an Oscar for her "unladylike" behavior on screen.

4   Katharine Hepburn, Ginger Rogers, and, of course, Terry Moore.

5   Jack Johnson. Before becoming an actor, McLaglen was a professional boxer (and wrestler) and fought a six-round exhibition match with Johnson in Vancouver, B.C.

6   The Ringo Kid, *Stagecoach* (1939); The Abilene Kid, *Three Godfathers* (1948); Kid Shelleen, *Cat Ballou* (1965); The Waco Kid, *Blazing Saddles* (1974).

7   Gary Cooper. Lasky was convinced that the only actor who could play York was Cooper, so he faked the telegram and sent it to the actor. Cooper was so impressed he took the lead in the film.

8   Kirk Douglas. He picked Kirk just because he liked the name. His real name is Issur Danielovitch.

9   Isaac Stern.

10  Dr. Joseph Goebbels. The first time he played the infamous war criminal was in 1939, in *Confessions of a Nazi Spy*.

ONLY IN HOLLYWOOD

# TWO OF A KIND
## Double Your Pleasure

1. Humphrey Bogart and Spencer Tracy, the two biggest male stars of their era, could never be brought together to make a film, in spite of their respect for one another. Why?

2. This world-famous duo first appeared together in a 1917 two-reeler and continued to team in films until their last in 1951.

3. What did the deaths of Bruce Lee and Jean Harlow have in common?

4. Why did J. Edgar Hoover request that Walt Disney change certain characters in two of his films?

5. The great comedy teams of Bob Hope and Bing Crosby and Dean Martin and Jerry Lewis "exchanged" cameo guest appearances in which two films?

6. In *To Have and Have Not* (1945), Humphrey Bogart's character calls Lauren Bacall's character Slim, even though her name is Marie. She in turn calls him Steve, when his name is actually Harry. Why?

7. During the censorship controversy over the film *The Outlaw* (1943), a Maryland trial judge protested that certain elements in the movie "hung over the picture like a thunderstorm spread over a landscape. They were everywhere." What was he describing?

8. Mae West usually had to have two versions of her costumes made for her films. Why?

9. This cinematic device was invented by George Spoor at RCA Victor's recording studios in New York.

10. Name Gene Kelly's unusual dance partner in a memorable scene from *Anchors Aweigh* (1945).

ANSWERS

# TWO OF A KIND
## Double Your Pleasure

1. Neither one would agree to give up—or somehow share—top billing on a picture.

2. Stan Laurel and Oliver Hardy. They did not know each other when they worked in the 1917 *Lucky Dog*, and did not begin to team up regularly until 1926.

3. Both died during the making of their last movies, and both films were finished using doubles, dubbing, and camera tricks. Lee's last film was *Game of Death* (1979) and Harlow's was *Saratoga* (1937).

4. Because the bumbling characters referred to as "federal security agents" in the movie *Moon Pilot* (1962) had originally been called FBI agents in the script. The same type of characters also appeared in *That Darned Cat* (1964).

5. Dean and Jerry appeared in Hope and Crosby's *The Road to Bali* (1952) and Bob and Bing returned the favor in Martin and Lewis's *Scared Stiff* (1953).

6. Director Howard Hawks put in this touch because his nickname for his wife Nancy was Slim and hers for him was Steve.

7. Jane Russell's breasts. Because she revealed too much cleavage, Hollywood censor Joe Breen objected to over one hundred scenes in the film.

8. Miss West's dresses were so tight she had to have one for standing and another version of the same dress made in a looser fashion for sitting and, more often, reclining.

9. The split lens.

10. Jerry, the cartoon mouse from Tom and Jerry fame.

# IN REAL LIFE
## Stranger than Fiction

1. The Laurel and Hardy silent *Big Business* (1929) ends with the team destroying a man's house (an actual house was used). What was ultimately embarrassing about the scene?

2. Who were the best man and the maid of honor at the first Liz Taylor–Richard Burton wedding?

3. The 1942 Academy Award–winning film *Mrs. Miniver* was received with great hostility by the people of Great Britain. Why?

4. The giant agency International Creative Management (ICM) went to binding arbitration over the rights to negotiate the deal for the sequel to this director's blockbuster hit of 1977.

5. Mystery writer Mickey Spillane played a couple of famous characters in *The Girl Hunters* (1963) and *Ring of Fear* (1954). What was unusual about each role?

6. The plot of this 1946 hard-boiled detective movie was so complex and convoluted that even director Howard Hawks later admitted, "I never figured out what was going on, but I thought that the basic thing had great scenes in it."

7. She rushed from the set of *Hotel Imperial* to the funeral of Rudolph Valentino, where she was photographed fainting.

8. Director King Vidor found it difficult to raise money to produce the film *Our Daily Bread* (1934). Why?

9. This former San Francisco madam was hired as a technical adviser on the 1965 film *Sylvia*.

10. Name the deadpan movie comic that started his career in vaudeville billed as The Human Mop.

ANSWERS

# IN REAL LIFE
## Stranger than Fiction

1. The shooting (and destruction) was done on location at the *wrong* house. The unlucky owners returned home that day to find it in a shambles.

2. Bob Wilson, Burton's black valet and dresser, was best man. Liz was unattended.

3. The movie was a romanticized look at a British family's involvement in World War II, and many angry people in England felt it was unrealistic and an embarrassment to them.

4. After *Star Wars*, George Lucas broke with the agency, who claimed it was still entitled to make the deal for the sequel *The Empire Strikes Back*. ICM lost.

5. He played his own literary creation, Mike Hammer, in *The Girl Hunters*, and played himself in *Ring of Fear*.

6. *The Big Sleep*. When Hawks asked Raymond Chandler, author of the original novel, to clarify who committed one of the story's murders, Chandler replied, "I don't know either."

7. Pola Negri. The press interpreted her actions as a ploy to get publicity.

8. During the depression, movie studios and banks were unwilling to finance films that dealt with the reality of the times. They thought a project such as Vidor's was doomed to failure. Vidor so believed in his movie that he mortgaged his home to pay for the film.

9. Sally Stanford.

10. Buster Keaton. Keaton's father tossed the child performer around the stage. This is where Keaton learned that he could get the best audience reaction by keeping a deadpan look on his face.

ONLY IN HOLLYWOOD

# ROMANCE HOLLYWOOD STYLE

1. What gift did Marlene Dietrich give to co-star Jimmy Stewart to win his affection when the two were making *Destry Rides Again* (1939)?

2. This actress's diary described the intimate details of her adulterous love affair with playwright George S. Kaufmann, and its contents helped to make for a titillating divorce trial.

3. Why did Lauren Bacall's father object to her marriage to Bogart?

4. Paul Newman said of this movie: "I don't think people realize what the picture was all about. It's a love affair between two men. The girl is incidental."

5. Name the comic genius who had a preference for young girls. His four marriages were to women aged sixteen, sixteen, twenty, and seventeen.

6. During a benefit in L.A. for victims of the 1937 Ohio River Flood, Ginger Rogers sold a kiss for $400. Who paid for the use of Ms. Rogers's lips?

7. While filming *The Charge of the Light Brigade* (1936), Errol Flynn was so taken with his co-star he played little tricks on her to win her affections. Who was she?

8. Actress Pier Angeli broke her engagement to this actor to marry singer Vic Damone.

9. Name the actress who shares a bed with sex bomb Raquel Welch in the movie *Myra Breckinridge* (1970).

10. When Rosalind Russell married Frederick (Freddie) Brisson in 1941, he was their best man.

ANSWERS
# ROMANCE HOLLYWOOD STYLE

1. She gave Stewart—who was an avid reader of Flash Gordon comics—a life-sized Flash Gordon doll that she had the studio art department create. The gift is said to have started their romance.

2. Mary Astor, who starred as the double-dealing temptress in *The Maltese Falcon* (1941).

3. Because of their age difference. He was forty-five and she was twenty.

4. *Butch Cassidy and the Sundance Kid* (1969) starring Newman, Robert Redford, and Katharine Ross. The movie was the biggest money-making western in history.

5. Charlie Chaplin.

6. Funnyman Harold Lloyd, who had outbid Cary Grant for the privilege.

7. Olivia de Havilland. One prank Flynn pulled was leaving a dead snake in Ms. de Havilland's panties. Understandably his advances were not reciprocated.

8. James Dean. Angeli and Dean met while filming *East of Eden* in 1954.

9. Farrah Fawcett.

10. Cary Grant. Grant was casually dating Russell and introduced her to her future mate.

## CAMEO ROLES
## Who Is That Masked Man?

1. Alfred Hitchcock's cameo appearances have been his trademark. In *Lifeboat* (1943), how did he manage to appear in spite of the fact that all the action took place on a small lifeboat adrift in the Atlantic Ocean?

2. Who appeared briefly in two early scenes of *The Treasure of the Sierra Madre* (1947), twice giving money to the same panhandler?

3. This legendary sex symbol appeared briefly in the Marx Brothers' *Love Happy* (1950), speaking one line to Groucho: "Mr. Grunion, I want you to help me . . . some men are following me." Who was she?

4. Columnist Hedda Hopper made a cameo appearance—as a columnist—in what classic film about Hollywood?

5. In *The Maltese Falcon* (1941), a man who has been shot staggers into Sam Spade's office carrying the falcon. Who was he and how was he "related" to the film?

6. Kevin McCarthy, star of this 1956 science-fiction classic, also appeared in one scene of the 1978 remake.

7. What well-known author appeared briefly in *Annie Hall* (1977) as a caricature of himself?

8. *It's a Mad Mad Mad Mad World* (1963) featured a cameo appearance by a famous comedy team of the thirties, forties, and fifties whose work enjoyed a renaissance of popularity in the 1980s. Who were they?

9. *The Tiger Makes Out* (1967), a comedy that starred Eli Wallach and Anne Jackson, included a forty-five-second cameo by a young New York stage actor who would soon become one of Hollywood's biggest stars. Who?

10. In what is probably the most bizarre cameo in movie history, a workman clad in cap and overalls wanders across the back of the sound stage during an elaborate musical production number in *Cain and Mabel* (1936). Why did this walk-on remain in the film?

ANSWERS

# CAMEO ROLES
## Who Is That Masked Man?

1. A character holds up a newspaper to reveal Hitchcock's photo in an advertisement—for a weight-loss product.

2. John Huston, directing himself as a character the script calls simply "a man in a white suit," helped out Humphrey Bogart with a few spare pesos.

3. Marilyn Monroe. Although it was her third film appearance, *Love Happy* was later advertised as "The Picture That Discovered Marilyn Monroe."

4. *Sunset Boulevard* (1950). She appears in the last scene on the telephone, dictating the "scoop" to her newspaper.

5. He was Walter Huston, father of the movie's director, John Huston.

6. *Invasion of the Body Snatchers*. In the latter, McCarthy shows up near the end pounding on passing cars and screaming, "They're here!"

7. Truman Capote. He is seen walking through Central Park, prompting Woody Allen's character to describe him as ". . . the winner of the Truman Capote look-alike contest."

8. The Three Stooges appear briefly in the film dressed as firemen.

9. Dustin Hoffman played a beatnik type in this, his very first film appearance.

10. By the time the workman was noticed—by the film editor—it was too late. He could not be cut without ruining the scene, and shooting the entire sequence over would have cost too much money.

# A Remarkable History

A REMARKABLE HISTORY

# THE SILENTS
## Seen and Not Heard

1. The original title of this silent epic was *The Clansman*.

2. What contribution did Walter Hovey, city editor of the *Chicago Tribune*, make to the movie industry?

3. He invented the first moving pictures, which were small film images that could be viewed in a box.

4. This director's prolific career began in 1925, when he directed the first of over twenty "two-reeler" western silent shorts, and continued to the 1970s.

5. Name the famous movie director who started his movie career as a technical advisor to D. W. Griffith.

6. At the ripe old age of sixteen, she wrote the script for *The New York Hat* (1912), Mary Pickford's last film produced by the Biograph studios.

7. What was a "chaser"?

8. Film audiences associate Boris Karloff with the monster in the movie version of the Frankenstein story, but when did the first Frankenstein play on the silver screen?

9. Name the famous movie director who is credited with the first camera close-up in movie history.

10. He headed up the Keystone Studio, which was the first company to sign Charlie Chaplin to a contract for the movies.

ANSWERS

# THE SILENTS
## Seen and Not Heard

1   *The Birth of a Nation* (1915), D. W. Griffith's classic. The movie told of the South's humiliation during Reconstruction. The film was very controversial and director Griffith was charged with racism.

2   Hovey is credited with coming up with the gimmick of the movie serial in 1913. To fend off fierce competition from local newspapers, he boosted sales by running a weekly thriller in his newspaper and the same story would be shown that week in the local movie houses. The first of these serials was called the *Tribune's The Adventures of Kathlyn* (1913).

3   Thomas Alva Edison invented "motion pictures" in the late nineteenth century. The viewing device was called a Kinetoscope.

4   William Wyler, who directed such classics as *Wuthering Heights* (1939), *The Best Years of Our Lives* (1946), and *Ben Hur* (1959), concluded his long career in 1970 with *The Liberation of L. B. Jones.*

5   Erich von Stroheim, an Austrian immigrant, played a host of Prussian officers in World War I movies before taking his place behind the camera.

6   Anita Loos.

7   In the early days of the cinema, the audience, trying to squeeze the most from their nickel entrance fee, would stay on for the second run of a movie. Managers hired husky men to encourage the patrons to leave the theater between films. The burly men became known as "chasers."

8   In 1910 Thomas Edison filmed a version of the classic horror film. Unfortunately the film has been lost to history.

9   D. W. Griffith is credited with the first close-up, although he did not originate the use of this camera angle. His role as an innovator cannot be underestimated; among other techniques he developed the long shot, the fade-out, many lighting techniques, parallel action, and rapid cutting.

10   Mack Sennett, who was at first unimpressed with the newcomer from England.

A REMARKABLE HISTORY

# SILENT STARS
## Mute Points

1. Star of von Stroheim's 1923 masterpiece *Greed*, this actress's life story, published after her death, is a combination candy cookbook and autobiography.

2. She was the "It" girl.

3. When this actor was hired by Triangle Film Company in 1915 for the starring role in *The Lamb*, he often disrupted the film with his antics and acrobatics.

4. This film cowboy based his movie character on frontier code—a good guy who was outside the law.

5. This popular costar of cowboy Tom Mix's films was known only by his first name. Who was he?

6. Who was Rodolpho Alfonzo Pierre Filibert Guglielmi di Valentina d'Antonguolla?

7. Name the actress whose extravagant movie wardrobe was said to have influenced the fashions of the twenties.

8. Name the stage actress who made her Hollywood debut with John Gilbert in *Man, Woman and Sin* (1927).

9. On his first tour of America in 1908 with the Karno Company, Charlie Chaplin was featured in an English review called "The Wow-Wows." His roommate on tour later became a noted star in his own right. Who was he?

10. Star of such classics as *Tess of the Storm Country* (1922), *Pollyanna* (1920), and *Little Annie Rooney* (1925), she claimed to be the first movie star.

ANSWERS

# SILENT STARS
## Mute Points

1. Zasu Pitts told her story in *Pitts' Hits* (1964).

2. Clara Bow. Author Madam Elinor Glyn, who had many of her romantic novels turned into movies, gave Bow the distinctive title. The "It" was nothing more than good old-fashioned sex appeal.

3. Douglas Fairbanks. Later in his film career his athletic tendencies came in handy with such films as *The Black Pirate* (1926), *The Iron Mask* (1929), and *Robin Hood* (1922).

4. William S. Hart. Hart was one of the few movie cowboys who had actually punched a cow in real life. He was raised in the then wilds of Wisconsin, when the state was populated with Sioux and Blackfeet Indians.

5. Mix's horse, Tony, probably the biggest star of all the movie horses.

6. Rudolph Valentino. After his initial success in *The Four Horsemen of the Apocalypse* (1921), Paramount signed Valentino for *The Sheik* (1921), the role with which he is still identified today.

7. Gloria Swanson in *Her Love Story* (1924). She wore a bridal dress estimated to cost $100,000.

8. Jeanne Eagels. The actress was a smash on Broadway as Sadie Thompson in *Rain*. Eagels despised making films, but it was through the movie industry that she achieved her greatest fame.

9. Stan Laurel.

10. Mary Pickford. Early films gave neither cast nor crew screen credits. While working for D. W. Griffith she was billed as The Biograph Girl or The Girl with the Golden Curls. As her popularity grew Pickford demanded that her name be advertised with the film. Once her name was billed, she became the first star.

A REMARKABLE HISTORY

# THE ACADEMY AWARDS
## Thank You, Thank You, Thank You

1. At the Fifth Annual Academy Awards in 1932, the membership was unable to decide which of two outstanding performances merited the Best Actor award. How did they resolve this problem?

2. When it was announced in 1973 that he would be presenting one of the major Oscars, it created such an uproar throughout Hollywood that the individual in question was forced to withdraw from the event. Who was he?

3. Which of the following won an Academy Award for Best Picture?
   a) *The Wizard of Oz* (1939).   b) *Citizen Kane* (1941).
   c) *Sunset Boulevard* (1950).   d) *Oliver!* (1968).   e) *Network* (1976).

4. Which of the following did not even receive an Academy Award *nomination* for Best Picture?
   a) *Rear Window* (1954).   b) *Some Like It Hot* (1959).
   c) *Cool Hand Luke* (1967).   d) *2001: A Space Odyssey* (1968).
   e) *Close Encounters of the Third Kind* (1977).

5. Robert Opel made Oscar history in 1974, but did not win any awards. What was his accomplishment?

6. This individual has won twenty-seven Academy Awards, more than anyone in the history of the Oscars.

7. What prompted the major studios to end their financial support for the Academy Awards presentation ceremony in 1948?

8. What 1977 film received eleven Academy Award nominations, but came up empty-handed on Oscar night?

9. At the Academy Awards presentation in 1978, Debbie Boone sang "You Light Up My Life" along with a group of girls interpreting the song in sign language for the deaf. How did this touching event later cause great embarrassment for the Academy?

10. Charlie Chaplin received only one Academy Award in his entire career. What was it for?

ANSWERS

# THE ACADEMY AWARDS
## Thank You, Thank You, Thank You

1. Two awards were given. One went to Fredric March for his performance in *Dr. Jekyll and Mr. Hyde* (a *dual* role, yet), and one to Wallace Beery for *The Champ.*

2. Mark Spitz, the former Olympics swimming champ. His representative at the William Morris Agency had wrangled the invitation for his client, but Hollywood felt Spitz simply had nothing to do with the movie business—other than the hope of breaking in himself.

3. *Oliver!* Go figure it out.

4. Not one of these films received a Best Picture nomination.

5. Opel managed to sneak backstage at the presentation ceremony, remove his tuxedo, and streak naked across the stage behind a startled David Niven, who then remarked: "Isn't it fascinating that probably the only laugh this man will ever get in his life is by stripping off his clothes and showing his shortcomings."

6. Walt Disney.

7. When it became apparent that Laurence Olivier's *Hamlet*, a British production, was easily going to win the Best Picture award, the studio executives decided they did not want to subsidize an event that would only publicize a foreign film. The awards ceremony struggled financially until 1952, when television saved the day.

8. *The Turning Point*, which starred Shirley MacLaine and Anne Bancroft. This record for futility was later equaled by Steven Spielberg's *The Color Purple* (1985).

9. Network switchboards were jammed with calls complaining that the sign language was inept. It was revealed that the girls were not really from a school for the deaf, as had been announced, but were simply recruited from a nearby high school.

10. At the very first awards banquet in 1929, Chaplin received a special award for "his genius and versatility in writing, acting, directing, and producing *The Circus* (1928).

A REMARKABLE HISTORY

# BLACKLISTING
## Are You Now or Have You Ever Been . . . ?

1. The director of *Wuthering Heights* (1939), *Ben Hur* (1959), and *Funny Girl* (1968) also helped form the Committee for The First Amendment (with John Huston and Phillip Dunne) in 1947 to combat investigations of Hollywood by the House Committee on Un-American Activities (HUAC). Who was he?

2. In 1948 the Screen Writers Guild attempted to end blacklisting by filing a suit against the Motion Picture Association of America, in which they charged the producers with collusion. Why was the suit dropped?

3. Writer Robert Rich won an Academy Award for his screenplay *The Brave One* in 1957. Why was he unable to appear at the ceremony to accept it?

4. Blacklisted screenwriter Ned Young won an Academy Award for *The Defiant Ones* (1957) while writing under the pseudonym of Nathan E. Douglas. What visual inside joke occurs during the film's opening credits?

5. The familiar phrase, "Are you now or have you ever been a member of the Communist Party?" was the *second* question the HUAC members asked the Hollywood Ten. What was the first question?

6. Why did actor Zero Mostel's imitation of "a butterfly at rest" get him into trouble with the House Committee on Un-American Activities?

7. What did Walt Disney, Jack Warner, Ronald Reagan, and Ginger Rogers's mother all have in common?

8. What was unusual about *The Front*, a 1976 film about the blacklist era that starred Woody Allen?

9. Who was the only one of the Hollywood Ten to recant?

10. Who was the Screen Actors Guild president who said, "We will not be party to a blacklist," just before the guild banned communists and noncooperative witnesses from membership?

ANSWERS

# BLACKLISTING
## Are You Now or Have You Ever Been . . . ?

1. William Wyler.

2. The guild became convinced that the very act of filing the suit would bring further charges of subversion and other attacks against them. It was withdrawn after the president of the producers' association, Eric Johnston, stated under oath that there was no blacklist . . . which the guild wrongly interpreted as a promise for the future.

3. Because Robert Rich did not exist. The name was a pseudonym used by Dalton Trumbo, who, as one of the Hollywood Ten, was being blacklisted for alleged communist sympathies.

4. Young appears briefly on screen while the credit for "Douglas" is shown.

5. "Are you now or have you ever been a member of the guild?" The question referred to the Screen Writers Guild or the Directors Guild.

6. Because he performed it at a benefit for *Mainstream*, a leftist political magazine. The committee accused him of ". . . putting money in the Communist Party coffers as a result of that urge to put a butterfly at rest."

7. All were "friendly witnesses" for the McCarthy hearings on communist activities in Hollywood, cooperating in naming co-workers they thought to have communist sympathies.

8. As the film's credits indicate, screenwriter Walter Bernstein, producer-director Martin Ritt, and five members of the cast—Zero Mostel, John Randolph, Lloyd Gough, Joshua Shelley, and Herschel Bernardi—had themselves all been victims of blacklisting.

9. Director Edward Dmytryk, after serving a six-month sentence for contempt, agreed to speak to the HUAC. The other nine, who did not change their minds, were Alvah Bessie, Herbert Biberman, Lester Cole, Ring Lardner, Jr., John Howard Lawson, Albert Maltz, Sam Ornitz, Adrian Scott, and Dalton Trumbo.

10. Ronald Reagan.

A REMARKABLE HISTORY

# SEQUELS AND REMAKES
## Once Is Not Enough

1. Which of the following was *not* a sequel:
   a) *Indiana Jones and the Temple of Doom* (1984).
   b) *The Empire Strikes Back* (1980).   c) *First Blood* (1982).
   d) *Magnum Force* (1973).   e) *For a Few Dollars More* (1967).

2. After winning an Oscar for his role in a 1938 film, Spencer Tracy played the same character in the less-popular 1941 sequel. What were the titles of both films?

3. How many films did the team of Dean Martin and Jerry Lewis appear in together?
   a) Four.   b) Seven.   c) Twelve.   d) Seventeen.

4. In spite of an all-star cast, this modern remake of a 1937 Frank Capra film became known in the industry as "Lost Investments," a heavy-handed reference to the nearly $10 million the movie lost.

5. *Son of Flubber* (1963) was Walt Disney's sequel to what earlier successful film?

6. Robert Montgomery as a boxer became Warren Beatty as a pro football player in the remake. What were the titles of the two films?

7. Acclaimed as one of the worst sequels in history, this 1977 film suckered in audiences for two weeks before word of mouth caused people to stay away in such numbers that the *Wall Street Journal* proclaimed: "Rarely, if ever, have box-office receipts declined so drastically."

8. Clark Gable starred in the original in 1932 and again in the remake in 1953. What were the two films' titles?

9. Actor Marlon Brando and writer Mario Puzo collaborated on two films. Each film had a sequel, and in each case, Puzo also worked on the sequel while Brando did not. One film was *The Godfather*. What was the other?

10. One steamy scene of this remake had Jessica Lange just rolling in dough, so to speak—something you could not have seen in the 1946 original.

# SEQUELS AND REMAKES
## Once Is Not Enough

1   *First Blood*, which marked the first appearance of (and led to the ... er, prequel called) Rambo.

2   *Boys' Town* (1938) and *Men of Boys' Town* (1941). Tracy played Father Flanagan in both.

3   Between 1949 and 1956 the team appeared in seventeen films, all for Paramount.

4   *Lost Horizon* (1973). Not Liv Ullmann, nor Peter Finch, nor songs by Burt Bacharach and Hal David were able to save this ill-advised remake.

5   *The Absent-Minded Professor* (1961). Both starred Fred MacMurray as Prof. Ned Brainard.

6   *Here Comes Mr. Jordan* (1941) was remade as *Heaven Can Wait* (1978).

7   *Exorcist II: The Heretic*.

8   *Red Dust* (1932) was remade as *Mogambo* (1953).

9   *Superman* (1978). Puzo also worked on the script of *Superman II* (1981), while Brando, after playing the Man of Steel's dad in *Superman*, did not get involved in the sequel.

10  *The Postman Always Rings Twice* (1981). Lana Turner's adultery was not nearly so graphic in the earlier version.

A REMARKABLE HISTORY

## ANDROGYNY
### Boys Will Be Girls, and Vice Versa

1. Marlene Dietrich started what nationwide trend in women's clothing in the early 1930s?

2. In his first professional *stage* appearance—before becoming a great movie tough guy—he played a female impersonator in a play titled *Every Sailor*.

3. Bette Davis once called this director "the male Bette Davis," and she meant it as a compliment.

4. Why did *Some Like It Hot* (1959) have to be shot in black-and-white instead of in color?

5. Name the only Cary Grant movie in which the suave actor appears in drag.

6. *East Side of Heaven* (1939) starred Bing Crosby and quite possibly the youngest male impersonator in films. Who was the child star?

7. Name the actress who won an Academy Award for her portrayal of a man in the movie *The Year of Living Dangerously* (1982).

8. Name the film in which Brian Aherne says to Katharine Hepburn, who is dressed as a boy, "There is something queer going on here."

9. Fashion designer Mr. Blackwell once said of this actor, "Better as a woman. If I were him, I'd never get out of drag." Who was Mr. Blackwell talking about?

10. At her only appearance at a Hollywood costume party, this legendary actress came dressed as Hamlet.

ANSWERS

# ANDROGYNY
## Boys Will Be Girls, and Vice Versa

1   Women wearing slacks became chic after Marlene's many on- and off-screen appearances in "man-drag."

2   James Cagney.

3   William Wyler, who directed Davis in *Jezebel* (1938), *The Letter* (1940), and *The Little Foxes* (1941).

4   Because when leading men Tony Curtis and Jack Lemmon were dressed as women, their feminine makeup made them look too garish and grotesque in color.

5   *I Was a Female War Bride* (1949). The plot takes a comic look at army regulations and has Grant donning a WAC uniform to marry Ann Sheridan.

6   Baby Sandy. One year old at the time, her ambiguous name made it possible for her to play both male and female roles.

7   Linda Hunt.

8   *Sylvia Scarlett* (1935). In the film Hepburn dons male clothes in order to escape from France.

9   The star of *Tootsie* (1983), Dustin Hoffman. There aren't many that agree with Mr. Blackwell.

10  Greta Garbo. Her costume was designed by Adrian. Garbo left the party when her picture was snapped by an unauthorized photographer.

A REMARKABLE HISTORY

# MARCHING OFF TO WORLD WAR II

1. What studio executive and producer of World War II films saw action firsthand as an army officer in North Africa and Western Europe during the war?

2. A 1942 Academy Award winner, *Der Fuehrer's Face*, starred one of America's most beloved entertainers. Who?

3. Acclaimed as one of the most moving documentaries of World War II, *The Battle of San Pietro* (1944) showed how Allied forces drove the Nazis from a strategically located Italian village. Who was its famous Hollywood director?

4. The first actual U.S.-combat film documentary, it won an Academy Award in 1942. What was it?

5. What circumstances made director Anatole Litvak take a very personal interest in his film, *Confessions of a Nazi Spy* (1939)?

6. Frank Capra, director of films such as *It Happened One Night* (1934) and *Mr. Smith Goes to Washington* (1939), produced a series of documentary films that attempted to answer the question "Why are Americans on the march?" What was the series called?

7. The great director John Ford, responsible for such classics as *Stagecoach* (1939) and *Fort Apache* (1948), made his first contribution to the war effort by directing an army training film of great interest to GIs overseas. What was it called?

8. How did humorist Robert Benchley help awaken America to the Nazi threat?

9. Harold Russell's only previous movie experience had been in an army training film called *Diary of a Sergeant* when he was selected to co-star in this 1946 Oscar-winning film.

10. Name the Hollywood actor who put his career in jeopardy by declaring himself a conscientious objector when he was inducted into the army during World War II.

ANSWERS

# MARCHING OFF TO WORLD WAR II

1. Darryl F. Zanuck of Twentieth Century-Fox was a colonel in the U.S. Army Signal Corps. Zanuck was responsible for two of the greatest World War II films ever made: *Twelve O'Clock High* (1949) and *The Longest Day* (1962).

2. Donald Duck. This satire on Nazism won its Oscar for Best Cartoon.

3. Maj. John Huston, whose other films have included *The Maltese Falcon* (1941), *The Treasure of the Sierra Madre* (1947), and, more recently, *Prizzi's Honor* (1985).

4. *The Battle of Midway* won the Oscar for short-subject (it ran twenty minutes) documentary. The director, John Ford, was wounded in the battle and later lost the use of his left eye because of the injury.

5. Litvak spent the early days of World War II in Europe being harassed by the German SS and Gestapo. He was producing films in France until just before the German invasion.

6. "Why We Fight." Capra also supervised the wartime series "Know Your Ally" and "Know Your Enemy." When he left the army in 1945, he was awarded the Distinguished Service Medal and the French Legion of Merit.

7. *Sex Hygiene* (1941), a thirty-minute film on the dangers of venereal disease. It was produced by Darryl F. Zanuck.

8. He co-wrote the script for Alfred Hitchcock's *Foreign Correspondent* (1940). The film, an attempt to counteract American isolationism, dealt with Nazi subversion in Europe just prior to the outbreak of the war.

9. *The Best Years of Our Lives.* Director William Wyler was so impressed with the physical and psychological adjustment by Russell, a handless former paratrooper, as portrayed in the documentary that he chose him for the role of Homer, the veteran whose hands have been replaced by hooks.

10. Lew Ayres. Ayres formed his pacifist beliefs while starring in the 1930 antiwar movie *All Quiet on the Western Front*.

A REMARKABLE HISTORY

# THE CRIMINAL ELEMENT
## You Dirty Rat!

1. The tough guy, who played the frightening killer Duke Mantee, stole the spotlight from stars Bette Davis and Leslie Howard in this 1936 film. Name the actor and the movie.

2. Al Capone is reputed to have enjoyed this gangster movie so much that he acquired his own print of it.

3. In which of the following did James Cagney *not* play the bad guy?
    a) *The Public Enemy* (1931).   b) *G-Men* (1935).
    c) *Angels with Dirty Faces* (1938).   d) *The Roaring Twenties* (1939).
    e) *White Heat* (1949).

4. The film that established Edward G. Robinson's bad-guy image ended with the bullet-riddled villain in the gutter asking the question: "Is this the end of Rico?" What was its title?

5. At age ten this future actor stole gym equipment from his Bronx school and hid the evidence in the caskets his father made for his livelihood. Who was the young juvenile delinquent?

6. On the night that this convicted murderer was executed in San Quentin, Marlon Brando was one of the many picketers outside the prison.

7. This actor, who first rose to fame in two of Hollywood's greatest bad-guy roles and went on to star in successful film biographies, had a strange weakness: a desire to buy something anytime he was in a stationery store.

8. This modern tough-guy hero can be glimpsed briefly next to Rita Hayworth in a scene from *Miss Sadie Thompson* (1954), but dominates the screen while shooting up assorted lowlifes in a series of three of the most violent films ever made.

9. This movie tough guy grew up in Manhattan's Hell's Kitchen and at one time was a driver for mobster Owney Madden.

10. On the night John Dillinger was shot in front of the Biograph Theater on Chicago's North Side, what movie was showing at the theater?

ANSWERS

# THE CRIMINAL ELEMENT
## You Dirty Rat!

1. Humphrey Bogart, in *The Petrified Forest*. Bogart was typecast in a series of gangster roles after this one.

2. *Scarface* (1932). Director Howard Hawks claimed that Capone praised the film when, at the gangster's request, the two met in Chicago.

3. Cagney was on the side of the law in *G-Men*.

4. *Little Caesar* (1931).

5. Sal Mineo. Once the caskets were delivered to the funeral home, his crime was discovered.

6. Caryl Chessman.

7. Paul Muni, whose roles included *Scarface* and *I Am a Fugitive from a Chain Gang* in 1932 and the lives of Louis Pasteur and Emile Zola in later films, would purchase pencils, rubber bands, paper clips, and notebooks for no apparent reason.

8. Charles Bronson, who was well-established as a tough guy long before his *Death Wish* trilogy.

9. George Raft. The actor was a compulsive gambler and lost his Hollywood fortune on bad bets. In 1960 he was fined by a federal judge for income-tax evasion.

10. MGM's *Manhattan Melodrama* (1934), starring Clark Gable, William Powell, and Myrna Loy.

A REMARKABLE HISTORY

# HOLLYWOOD AND THE WHITE HOUSE

1 What president subscribed to the *Hollywood Reporter* while in the White House?

2 Ronald Reagan's last movie, in 1964, was a remake of a 1946 film that helped to launch Burt Lancaster's career. What was its title?

3 While he was governor of Georgia, this president-to-be invited Robert Aldrich and Burt Reynolds to the governor's mansion to insure them of the state's cooperation during the filming of *The Longest Yard* (1974).

4 On what film did Eleanor Roosevelt call the producer with casting advice?

5 Who was the first U.S. president to be filmed for the silver screen?

6 About this film, President Woodrow Wilson said, "It is like writing history with lightning and my one regret is that it is all so terribly true."

7 This president was depicted in Africa hunting lions in a 1910 film.

8 According to director Otto Preminger, this actress almost became Mrs. John Fitzgerald Kennedy.

9 Name the movie that inspired John W. Hinckley, Jr. to make an assassination attempt on President Ronald Reagan.

10 In 1970 J. Edgar Hoover had a fake letter sent to a Tinsel Town columnist alleging that this actress threatened to kill President Nixon.

ANSWERS

# HOLLYWOOD AND THE WHITE HOUSE

1. Franklin D. Roosevelt had an airmailed copy on his desk each day.

2. *The Killers.*

3. Jimmy Carter.

4. *The Man Who Came to Dinner* (1941). She called Hal Wallis to insist that only Orson Welles could play the lead. The role eventually went to Monty Woolley.

5. William McKinley was filmed campaigning for the presidency in 1896 by the Biograph Company.

6. *The Birth of a Nation* (1915), D. W. Griffith's epic film about the South during Reconstruction. This was the first film to be shown in the White House.

7. Teddy Roosevelt. Many moviegoers thought they were watching a documentary, when in fact the producer, Col. William Selig, shot the film in his Chicago studio using an actor.

8. Gene Tierney. The Kennedy family did not think the actress was a suitable mate for the future President. She did marry Oleg Cassini, who would later design First Lady Jackie Kennedy's inaugural gown.

9. *Taxi Driver* (1976). In the movie Travis Bickle (Robert De Niro) is unsuccessful in his attempt to assassinate presidential candidate Charles Palatine.

10. Jane Fonda. She was never popular in conservative political circles. During the 1972 Republican Convention a petition was circulated calling for her trial for treason.

A REMARKABLE HISTORY

# BLACK HOLLYWOOD
## Soul on Celluloid

1. Name the first "black film" with a black director.

2. The movie *Watermelon Man* (1970) featured an unusual Hollywood first. What was it?

3. Who said, "The only choice permitted us is either to be servants for $7 a week or portray them for $700 per week"?

4. The NAACP called for a boycott of this 1947 Walt Disney film.

5. Discovered by MGM at the Mocambo Club in Hollywood, she was the first black female vocalist with an all-white band.

6. In 1931 Ronald Colman and Helen Hayes starred in a film version of Sinclair Lewis's *Arrowsmith*. Clarence Brooks, a black actor, was cast in an unusual role in the film. What was it?

7. This 1929 Fox release was billed as the first all-Negro musical.

8. Name the movie that featured blues singer Bessie Smith in her first and only film appearance.

9. What did Shirley Temple, Zasu Pitts, Al Jolson, Marion Davies, Fred Astaire, Mickey Rooney, Judy Garland, Paul Muni, and the puppet Charlie McCarthy have in common?

10. This 1963 film was shot in fourteen days and all the cast members worked for salaries below their standard fees. Why?

ANSWERS

# BLACK HOLLYWOOD
## Soul on Celluloid

1. *Cotton Comes to Harlem* (1970), directed by Ossie Davis. Davis was criticized by the black community for making a comedy about the New York ghetto when militant issues needed to be addressed.

2. Its star, Godfrey Cambridge, wore white face in a turn-about-is-fair-play on the black face that white actors had affected for years in films.

3. Hattie McDaniel, who was the first black person to win an Academy Award. She won the Oscar for playing a maid in *Gone With the Wind* (1939).

4. *Song of the South*, an adaptation of the Uncle Remus stories that showed the happy slaves on the master's plantation.

5. Lena Horne. Her first movie role was in *Panama Hattie* (1942).

6. Brooks played a medical doctor, which in the 1930s was quite a departure from the usual maid and song-and-dance roles reserved for black actors. Unfortunately, the movie was not a financial success, or perhaps Hollywood would have been more generous with its roles for black actors.

7. *Hearts in Dixie*, starring Clarence Muse, Mildred Washington, and Stepin Fetchit. It was a stereotypical movie of the carefree life of blacks on a southern plantation.

8. *St. Louis Blues* (1928).

9. They all appeared in black face at one time or another in the movies.

10. *Lilies of the Fields* did not have the usual big Hollywood budget and the actors considered working on the project as a labor of love. Star Sidney Poitier garnered an Oscar for his efforts in the film.

# CENSORSHIP
## You Can't Say/Show/Do That!

1. The 1936 film *These Three* was adapted from Lillian Hellman's play of a different title. What was the play's title and why was it changed?

2. What then-shocking scene was snipped from the 1934 *Tarzan and His Mate*?

3. This film classic was banned in Minneapolis, Chicago, Boston, Pittsburgh, St. Louis, and Denver in 1915, because many people felt it would foster hatred between blacks and whites.

4. In *Splendor in the Grass* (1961), Natalie Wood's character is arguing with her mother when she jumps up and runs down the hall to her bedroom. What made this scene subject to censorship?

5. When New York's Cardinal Spellman said, "It is the moral and patriotic duty of every local citizen to defend America from dangers which threaten our beloved country from beyond our boundaries, but also the dangers which confront us at home," what dangers "at home" was he talking about?

6. Because of a local ordinance in Kenosha, Wisconsin, children under eighteen were denied entry to this R-rated documentary even when accompanied by their parents.

7. A love scene containing some questionable monkeying around was cut from this 1933 classic film, but later restored in 1971. What was the movie?

8. Will H. Hays was appointed by the major studio heads to police the morals of the movie industry. At the time of the appointment, he had another job that occupied his time. What was it?

9. William Randolph Hearst's chain of newspapers refused to carry any advertising for this 1941 film.

10. Central Casting, through which aspiring actors could find employment as extras in movies, was originally created for what purpose?

ANSWERS

# CENSORSHIP
## You Can't Say/Show/Do That!

1. The play, *The Children's Hour*, touched on the subject of lesbianism—taboo in Hollywood at the time—so the film could neither use the original title nor make reference to the play in its advertising. It was eventually remade (faithful to the play in title and content) in 1962.

2. When Tarzan (Johnny Weissmuller) and Jane (Maureen O'Sullivan) go swimming, Jane rises from the water with one of her breasts exposed. Censors and citizens' groups complained, and MGM cut the scene.

3. *The Birth of a Nation* (1915). Later, the NAACP also tried to prevent its showing in various parts of the country.

4. Natalie was in a bathtub during the argument. When she runs down the hall we see her bare backside, which caused both Hollywood censors and the Catholic Legion of Decency to object, so the scene was cut.

5. *Baby Doll* (1956), Elia Kazan's film based on a play by Tennessee Williams. Spellman urged Catholics not to see the film "under penalty of sin." In France it was then advertised as "Condemned by Cardinal Spellman," which helped to bring in the Catholic crowds.

6. *Woodstock* (1970). The adults got a federal district court injunction against the local law, claiming it denied their children rights of freedom of expression.

7. *King Kong*. A scene in which the big ape peels off Fay Wray's clothes was one of several cut and later restored to the film over the years. A grisly sequence involving some giant man-eating spiders, however, has not been seen since 1933.

8. Hays, a Presbyterian elder, was postmaster general of the United States under President Harding.

9. Orson Welles's *Citizen Kane*. The movie is reputed to be the thinly veiled story of Hearst.

10. Will H. Hays created the agency in order to scrutinize the moral conduct of actors applying to work in the motion-picture business.

A REMARKABLE HISTORY

# THAT'S WHEN HOLLYWOOD KNEW HOW TO THROW A PARTY!

1. How did Sheilah Graham and F. Scott Fitzgerald meet?

2. Hollywood's grandest party of 1935 was thrown by Carole Lombard at what popular amusement area?

3. Name the Hollywood couple who at the height of the Great Depression gave a Christmas party at their home that featured the following accouterments: hundreds of Christmas trees covered with artificial snow and illuminated in blue light, a horse-drawn sleigh pulled across a driveway covered with snow made of untoasted corn flakes and paraffin, and a rosy-cheeked chorus of choirboys singing carols.

4. Some of the most legendary Hollywood parties of the thirties took place not in L.A., but farther up the California coast at San Simeon. Who gave the parties?

5. Douglas Fairbanks and Mary Pickford, known as The King and Queen of Hollywood, would often entertain real royalty at their home, Pickfair. When a duke and duchess were served dinner, Doug and Mary relaxed a house rule. What was the house rule put aside for visitors of noble birth?

6. A tragic "Hollywood" party took place at the St. Francis Hotel in San Francisco on September 5, 1921. What were the circumstances?

7. When Countess Dorothy di Frasso left Hollywood to move back to Rome, she threw a lavish costume ball. What was her connection to the film community?

8. When this movie was premiered in Atlanta, the mayor encouraged the city's men to grow sideburns and goatees and the women to don hooped skirts.

9. At this silent-film director's parties, a servant would sound a gong at eleven o'clock and the faint of heart were warned to take their leave.

10. According to her private secretary, Daisy Devoe, this actress spent an amorous weekend with the USC football team.

ANSWERS

# THAT'S WHEN HOLLYWOOD KNEW HOW TO THROW A PARTY!

1. At a party at Robert Benchley's Garden of Allah bungalow.

2. The Venice Pier. Lombard had the area closed to the public for her bash, and she and her Hollywood cronies had the rides and arcades all to themselves.

3. Basil and Ouida Rathbone.

4. William Randolph Hearst and his lover Marion Davies. Their guest list read like the who's who of Hollywood: Clark Gable, Carole Lombard, Irene Dunne, Bette Davis, Claudette Colbert, Dolores del Rio, Norma Shearer, Merle Oberon, Cary Grant, Randolph Scott, Leslie Howard, Jean Harlow, Henry Fonda, David Niven, and Tyrone Power were among the notables who attended their many parties.

5. The Fairbanks never served alcohol at their rather staid Hollywood affairs. They made an exception in the case of royalty.

6. Comedian Fatty Arbuckle was accused of killing actress Virginia Rappe in a drunken orgy. He was later acquitted in a jury trial, but the bad press he had received ruined his acting career.

7. The countess was Gary Cooper's paramour. She met Cooper in Italy, followed him to California, and left when Cooper married socialite Veronica Balfe.

8. *Gone With the Wind* (1939). The mayor also declared a three-day festival surrounding the movie's opening.

9. Mack Sennett. After eleven all hell would break loose: actors and actresses chased each other through the director's estate, and when they caught each other, their sexual exploits would have made a Keystone Kop blush.

10. The silent screen's Clara Bow did "it" with the entire team.

A REMARKABLE HISTORY

# TRADEMARKS
## One(s) of a Kind

1. John Barrymore left more than his handprints in the cement outside Grauman's Chinese Theater. Of what did he leave an imprint?

2. Groucho Marx was told to discard his trademark black-greasepaint moustache (he had worn it for years on stage) for the Marx Brothers' first film, *The Coconuts* (1929). Why?

3. This studio trademark actually makes a "cameo appearance" in the scenes of a Bob Hope–Bing Crosby road picture.

4. Jane Fonda is almost as well-known for working out in a leotard as she is for acting in her movies. Before she became the physical fitness queen of Hollywood, what disease did she suffer from as a teenager?

5. Name the actress who is quoted as saying, "I never did cheesecake. I just used my hair."

6. Joan Crawford claimed she had weak ankles that needed support. As a result these became her trademark.

7. Bette Davis's imitators often say, "Petah, Petah, Petah," while puffing on a cigarette. In which film did Davis play opposite a Peter?
   a) *All About Eve* (1950).   b) *Hollywood Canteen* (1944).
   c) *The Little Foxes* (1941).   d) *Dark Victory* (1939).

8. Name the superstar whose trademark off-balance gait was the result of a car accident in his teenage years in Montana.

9. In the first decade of the twentieth century, producers inserted their trademarks in each scene of their films. Why?

10. The movie *The Big Broadcast of 1938* was notable in Bob Hope's career in what way?

ANSWERS

# TRADEMARKS
## One(s) of a Kind

1  His profile.

2  The movie people feared that it looked too phony on the screen and audiences wouldn't believe it. Groucho replied, "The audience doesn't believe us, anyhow," and kept it for his entire movie career.

3  The Paramount "mountain" is seen in *The Road to Utopia* (1945), and prompts an appropriate remark from Hope.

4  Bulimia, a condition in which sufferers go on food binges and then purge themselves through self-induced vomiting.

5  Veronica Lake, who is probably best remembered for her blond hair draped over one eye.

6  High-heeled shoes with plastic ankle straps.

7  None of the above. Davis never uttered the often-mimicked line in any of her movies. Arthur Blake first used the line to parody Davis.

8  Gary Cooper. While driving a Model T with a friend, the brakes failed, Coop was thrown from the car, and it rolled over onto his hip. His injured hip never fully recovered.

9  In those days pirates could copy the film negative, insert their own titles, and release the movie as their own. To protect against this practice, a producer displayed his trademark in each scene of the film.

10  It was in this film that Hope sang what was to become his theme song, "Thanks for the Memory."

A REMARKABLE HISTORY

# SONG AND DANCE
## That's (Not Always) Entertainment

1. Clint Eastwood sang "I Talk to the Trees But They Don't Listen to Me" and Lee Marvin sang "I Was Born Under a Wand'rin' Star" in this 1969 musical.

2. The movie *Friendly Persuasion* (1956) featured a song called "Marry Me, Marry Me" that was recorded by the star of the movie. It was his first—and only—record. Who was he?

3. Which of the following did *not* dance in a movie with Fred Astaire?
    a) Leslie Caron.   b) Judy Garland.   c) Cyd Charisse.
    d) Debbie Reynolds.   e) Ginger Rogers.

4. The song "I Can't Begin to Tell You," from the film *The Dolly Sisters* (1945), was recorded by a singer named Ruth Haig. What was unusual about her?

5. In *To Have and Have Not* (1945), the vocal on Lauren Bacall's song with Hoagy Carmichael was originally dubbed by a better-known singer. Who?

6. In the movie *Valley of the Dolls* (1967), Susan Hayward sang "I'll Plant My Own Tree." For whom was the song originally written?

7. The Oscar-winning *Amadeus* (1984) starred the relatively unknown F. Murray Abraham and Tom Hulce in the leads. Studio executives had initially wanted to cast two better-known actors in the roles. Who?

8. Featured in the film *This Is the Army* (1943), this song was written in 1917 but remained unpublished until 1938, because the composer thought it was excessively patriotic.

9. Name the teen-heartthrob recording star who wrote the theme song for the World War II flick *The Longest Day* (1962).

10. *Carefree* (1938) was the only RKO film starring Fred Astaire in which he was neither a musician nor a dancer. What was his profession in the film?

ANSWERS

# SONG AND DANCE
## That's (Not Always) Entertainment

1  *Paint Your Wagon*, a disaster that Eastwood says convinced him to start producing and directing his own movies.

2  Gary Cooper.

3  Debbie Reynolds, though she *did* dance with Gene Kelly. Fred's other dance partners: Caron in *Daddy Long Legs* (1955), Garland in *Easter Parade* (1948), Charisse in *Silk Stockings* (1957), Rogers . . . no explanation is necessary.

4  Ruth Haig was a pseudonym for actress Betty Grable, who starred in the picture. The name was used because her contract forbade her to make recordings.

5  Andy Williams. They were unable to find a female singer with a voice as low as Bacall's. Her own voice was finally used in the film, when it was determined that her singing wasn't all that bad.

6  Judy Garland, who was originally slated to be in the movie that paralleled her own tragic life.

7  Burt Reynolds as Salieri and Timothy Hutton as Mozart. The execs thought that a classical music drama would not be a box-office success without established stars. Director Milos Forman felt just the opposite.

8  Irving Berlin's "God Bless America." All the earned royalties went into a trust fund established by Berlin for the Boy Scouts and Girl Scouts of America.

9  Paul Anka, who was also featured in the film, as were rock idols Fabian and Tommy Sands.

10  He played Tony Flagg, psychiatrist.

## HORROR
## "You Must Be Mad, Doctor . . ."

1. This director of sophisticated fright films is the son of a surgeon, which, he has said, may account for his high tolerance of blood.

2. Name the famous 1968 low-budget horror film—shot in Pittsburgh—that inspired a 1979 sequel by director George Romero.

3. A pioneer of the horror film, he ran away from school and joined a traveling circus for several years before directing the original *Dracula* (1931) and the macabre (all but two of the actors are physically deformed) *Freaks* (1932).

4. This modern master director of B horror movies claims his real wish would be: "Send me back to the forties and the studio system and let me direct movies."

5. Star of *Mad Love* (1935), *The Face Behind the Mask* (1941), and *The Beast with Five Fingers* (1946), he once studied under Alfred Adler and Sigmund Freud.

6. Name the 1931 horror movie in which the featured player was not listed in the film's credits.

7. Three actors have portrayed Quasimodo in film versions of *The Hunchback of Notre Dame*. Who were they?

8. This horror film star received his master's degree in fine arts from the University of London in 1935.

9. In this Vincent Price movie a skeletal figure would fly from the screen across the movie theater with the aid of a wire.

10. Name the comedy in which Raymond Massey would become outraged if anyone commented on the fact he resembled the horror-film star Boris Karloff.

ANSWERS

# HORROR
## "You Must Be Mad, Doctor..."

1. Brian De Palma let the blood flow in *Carrie* (1976) and the sophistication show in *Dressed to Kill* (1980).

2. *Night of the Living Dead* remains a classic. The later *Dawn of the Dead* er, ... pales by comparison.

3. Tod Browning. In keeping with the bizarre nature of his films, Browning's death was erroneously announced in 1944—though he lived until 1962.

4. John Carpenter, best known for *Halloween* (1978), *The Fog* (1980), and the remake of *The Thing* (1982), among others.

5. Peter Lorre was a pupil of the founders of the then-new field of psychiatry, but decided that acting was his first love. His first movie role was that of a psychotic child murderer in the German film *M*.

6. *Frankenstein*. Boris Karloff's name was not included in the screen credits. Instead the part was listed as The Monster: ?, because executives at Universal thought it would be a great publicity stunt for the movie. Karloff had to wait a full year before it was revealed that he had played the monster.

7. Lon Chaney (1923), Charles Laughton (1939), and Anthony Quinn (1957).

8. Vincent Price. He was appointed to the Fine Arts Committee of the White House and to the Latin Arts and Crafts Board of the U.S. Department of the Interior. Price put his knowledge of art to the test when he was a winning contestant on "The $64,000 Question" in 1956.

9. *The House on Haunted Hill* (1959). Director William Castle called this device Emergo. It failed to terrify audiences across the country.

10. *Arsenic and Old Lace* (1944). Karloff had been originally scheduled to play the Massey role of the deranged brother Jonathan.

# SECONDS
## Not-So-Terrible Twos

1. The first time the word "damn" is heard on the silver screen is in *Gone With the Wind* (1939), but can you name the second film to use the four-letter word?

2. What was the first picture to sweep all five major Academy Awards, winning for Best Picture, Best Actor, Best Actress, Best Director, and Best Screenplay (Adaptation)?

3. MGM art director Cedric Gibbons's long list of movie credits will probably always be overshadowed by his one other very famous achievement. What is it?

4. *Star Wars* was the highest-grossing film in 1977. Which was the second-highest grossing film that year?

5. What did Hollywood couples Liz Taylor and Richard Burton and Natalie Wood and Robert Wagner have in common?

6. Only one sequel has ever won the Oscar for Best Picture, and in doing so matched the achievement of the original two years earlier.

7. This sequel was not produced until twenty-three years after the original terrified audiences in 1960, though it did star the same actor.

8. When this 1932 Hemingway movie was released it had two endings and each exhibitor could decide which he preferred. Name the film with the choice of endings.

9. Although he was only on the screen for seven minutes, this actor won an Oscar for Best Supporting Actor in *Lust for Life* (1956).

10. Name actress Sally Blane's famous sibling.

ANSWERS

# SECONDS
## Not-So-Terrible Twos

1. *On the Waterfront* (1954). Marlon Brando uses the offensive word on a priest.

2. *It Happened One Night* (1934) won honors for Clark Gable, Claudette Colbert, director Frank Capra, and writer Robert Riskin. This feat was not duplicated until *One Flew Over the Cuckoo's Nest* won the same five awards in 1975.

3. He designed the Oscar statuette.

4. *Smokey and the Bandit*, starring Burt Reynolds and Sally Field. The film's domestic receipts topped $200 million.

5. Each couple was married twice. Wood and Wagner married in 1957, divorced in 1962, and remarried in 1972. Taylor and Burton married in 1964, divorced in 1974, remarried in 1975, and divorced again in 1976.

6. *The Godfather, Part II* (1974) and *The Godfather* (1972) were the only pair to both win Best Picture.

7. *Psycho II* brought back Anthony Perkins in the title role as an older—but no saner—Norman Bates.

8. *A Farewell to Arms*. In one ending Catherine dies on screen and in the other a fadeout occurs just before her untimely death.

9. Anthony Quinn, who played the artist Paul Gauguin.

10. Loretta Young.

# Behind the Scenes

BEHIND THE SCENES

# SPECIAL EFFECTS
## How'd They Do That?

1. In *The Birds* (1963), when Melanie (Tippi Hedren) is viciously attacked by birds in the attic, which of the following were used?
    a) Mechanical birds.  b) Live birds.  c) Animation-generated birds.

2. These famous weapons were actually fiber glass rods coated with a highly reflective material.

3. When Dr. Spock went to the planet Vulcan in *Star Trek: The Motion Picture* (1979), what popular tourist spot was he actually visiting?

4. This famous chandelierlike spacecraft was actually built of Plexiglas, steel, fiber glass, plywood, and aluminum tubes carrying high-voltage wires, encircled by neon tubes.

5. The "dueling skeletons" scenes from *The Seventh Voyage of Sinbad* (1958) and *Jason and the Argonauts* (1963) were achieved through the use of:
    a) Life-sized marionettes.  b) Miniature models.
    c) Actors in skeleton costumes.  d) Mirrors and light projection.

6. When the original *King Kong* (1933) is attacked by airplanes while atop the Empire State Building, which of the following do we not actually see on screen?
    a) Model airplanes.  b) Animation-generated planes.
    c) Real planes.  d) The real Empire State Building.

7. In *The Exorcist* (1973), Regan (Linda Blair) turns her head almost completely around to face backward. What *really* moved?
    a) Her body.  b) Her head.  c) Both.  d) Neither.

8. In *The Ten Commandments* (1956), how did Cecil B. DeMille get the Red Sea to part?

9. In *The Godfather* (1972), Sonny Corleone (James Caan) is riddled with bullets at a toll booth (perhaps he didn't have exact change?). Before the scene, Caan actually looked a bit like a telephone switchboard. Why?

10. Three full-scale (twenty-five-foot) mechanical sharks were used in *Jaws* (1975). How many crew members did it take to operate one of them?
    a) Four.  b) Nine.  c) Fifteen.  d) Twenty.

ANSWERS

# SPECIAL EFFECTS
## How'd They Do That?

1. Live trained birds were thrown at Hedren by two men off-camera, and for part of the sequence, some birds were tied to her with nylon threads so they wouldn't fly away! Shooting would stop every few seconds so her clothing could be torn and "blood" painted on her skin.

2. The "laser swords" used in *Star Wars* (1977). Light was reflected onto the rods by mirrors in front of the camera lens (a process called "front projection"), and the color was later enhanced by animation.

3. Yellowstone National Park. A matte painting of a reddish Vulcan landscape was photographed and that film combined with the live action in a composite shot.

4. The alien ship that descended in *Close Encounters of the Third Kind* (1977) was an oval of lights six feet in diameter. Two other models were also built to show the ship opening and at rest.

5. Miniature models. Each model's movements were synchronized with those of the actor with whom it "dueled," and then photographed in stop-motion animation and composited into the live-action footage.

6. Animation-generated planes. Shots of real biplanes flying over the real New York were intercut with those of wire-suspended models photographed against paintings of New York City.

7. Both her head and her body. Blair sat in a swivel chair and a body cast was attached to her at the neck. The fake body remained stationary while, inside it, she spun around in the chair.

8. With composite photography. Shots of the actual Red Sea were matched with footage of water poured from giant tanks at the studio. By reversing the film of the pouring water and combining it with film of the real sea, the waters appeared to part.

9. His body was covered with thin wires, each attached to a tiny metal plate that was rigged with an explosive charge and "blood" capsule. When the wires were touched to an off-camera battery, the explosive caps were detonated. The same technique had been used in *Bonnie and Clyde* (1967).

10. Fifteen. Each shark could be made to lash its tail, wave its fins, dive, surface, bite, chew, and roll its eyes. Two were attached to an underwater platform and the other to a submerged sledlike mechanism.

BEHIND THE SCENES

# TAKING A CHANCE
## No Guts, No Glory

1. How did Katharine Hepburn and Spencer Tracy meet?

2. What was the first full-length cartoon?

3. When the bridge was blown up in *The Bridge on the River Kwai* (1957), the effect was achieved with:
    a) A miniature model.
    b) Composite photography and painted mattes.
    c) Animation.   d) An actual bridge being blown up.

4. In 1942, she became the first woman to be elected president of the Academy of Motion Picture Arts and Sciences.

5. In her biography, *The Beauty and the Billionaire*, this actress claims Howard Hughes and she were married in 1949 aboard a yacht near Mexico.

6. This film was probably the most successful in Hollywood history in terms of revenues over cost, grossing over $117 million after being produced for just $750,000.

7. Although the odds were not in his favor, Marlon Brando took a chance in January 1986 that paid off at 1,000 to 1. What was it?

8. When Alan Ladd, Jr., president of Twentieth Century-Fox, budgeted $9 million for a science-fiction movie, many thought he'd lose his shirt. What was the controversial movie?

9. When he bought the rights to the book *One Flew Over the Cuckoo's Nest* in 1962, this actor thought he would one day play the lead role of Randle McMurphy on the silver screen.

10. Executives at Warner Brothers were having financial difficulties and took a gamble on this unusual first-time-only film.

ANSWERS

# TAKING A CHANCE
## No Guts, No Glory

1. MGM allowed Hepburn to select her male co-star for *Woman of the Year* (1942). She admired Tracy's performances in *Captains Courageous* (1937) and *Dr. Jekyll and Mr. Hyde* (1941) and asked to work with him, thus beginning a twenty-five-year professional and romantic relationship.

2. *Snow White and the Seven Dwarfs* (1938). A Walt Disney production, of course.

3. A real bridge was built and blown up with a real train crossing it.

4. Bette Davis. She resigned her post when she discovered she was expected to be only a figurehead.

5. Terry Moore.

6. *American Graffiti* (1973), by George Lucas, was a low-budget special compared to his 1977 *Star Wars*.

7. Brando purchased a $1 ticket in the California State Lottery that paid off at $1,000.

8. The blockbuster hit *Star Wars* (1977). The young Ladd also had an eye for other hits in the seventies: *Julia* (1977), *The Turning Point* (1977), and *Norma Rae* (1979).

9. Kirk Douglas, who played McMurphy on Broadway, turned the rights over to his son Michael. The movie swept the Oscars in 1975: Best Picture, Best Actor, Best Actress, Best Director, and Best Screenplay (Adaptation).

10. *The Jazz Singer* (1927), the first talking picture. The play, starring George Jessel, had run for three years on Broadway when Warner Brothers bought the rights for the screen. Al Jolson was given the lead in the movie because he had invested heavily in this novel venture.

BEHIND THE SCENES

# SETS AND LOCATIONS
## This Must Be the Place

1. What did the sets of *Sunset Boulevard* and *Rebel Without a Cause* have in common?

2. Which of the following served as the Holy Land in the filming of *The Greatest Story Ever Told* (1965)?
   a) Wahweap, Arizona.   b) Lake Moab, Utah.
   c) Death Valley, California.   d) Pyramid Lake, Nevada.
   e) Hollywood's Desilu Studio back lot.

3. Why did the set of *The Conqueror* (1956), a movie about Genghis Khan, turn out to be the most dangerous in movie history?

4. When *Doctor Dolittle* (1968) was being shot on location in Castle Combe, England, one of the local residents was angered that the film production was disrupting the lives of the local citizenry. How did he express his displeasure?

5. When *Heaven's Gate* (1981) director Michael Cimino was refused permission to shoot a scene on location at Harvard, what school did he use as a substitute?

6. This 1955 epic's advertising pitch was "Filmed in Egypt by the largest location crew ever sent abroad from Hollywood," claiming cast and crew totaled 21,000.

7. The only Hollywood film made on location in Iran was financed by the Shah himself, in one of his last official mistakes before being deposed.

8. *The Blue Bird* (1976), a little-known, star-studded spectacular whose cast included Elizabeth Taylor, Jane Fonda, Ava Gardner, and Cicely Tyson, was filmed on location in what unlikely place?

9. In *The Russians Are Coming! The Russians Are Coming!* (1966), the geography of Maine, where the story is set, is altered in what unusual way?

10. While on location on Catalina Island, technical advisor Father Lord would say Mass each morning before the day's filming would begin on this movie.

ANSWERS

# SETS AND LOCATIONS
## This Must Be the Place

1. The swimming pool used in the opening scene of *Sunset Boulevard* (1950) was the same one that James Dean, Natalie Wood, and Sal Mineo played at the bottom of in *Rebel Without a Cause* (1955). It was part of a Hollywood mansion owned by a former wife of J. Paul Getty.

2. All of them.

3. Part of it was filmed on location in the Utah desert, less than 150 miles from an atomic test site in Nevada. Since then, almost half of the 220 cast and crew members have contracted some radiation-related illness, and close to 50 have died.

4. He set off a homemade bomb under a temporary sandbag dam the movie crew had built to block the local river, in the hope that it would flood the set and destroy their equipment. The film, despite this act, was completed.

5. Oxford University in England. It cost almost $4 million to do the scene, which occupied about ten minutes of on-screen time.

6. *Land of the Pharaohs*, which also used sixteen hundred camels and one twenty-two-year-old Joan Collins.

7. *Caravans* (1978), an adaptation of a James Michener novel, starring Anthony Quinn and Jennifer O'Neill.

8. Leningrad. The movie was a special joint Soviet-American production that— you should pardon the expression—bombed.

9. Eucalyptus trees, which do not grow in Maine, are seen along the coast. It was actually shot in northern California.

10. Cecil B. DeMille's *The King of Kings* (1927). Other technical advisors on the biblical epic were the Reverend William Barton and the Reverend George Reid Andrews of the Federal Council of Churches.

BEHIND THE SCENES

# HOLLYWOOD MYTHS
## Don't Believe All You Hear

1. Although *The Jazz Singer* (1927) is always acclaimed as the first "talkie" because it featured synchronized songs and some synchronized dialogue, it was not the first "all-talking" sound picture. What was?

2. Samuel Goldwyn, author of many legendary malaproprisms, is often credited with the quote, "It rolls off my back like a duck." He didn't really say it. Who did?

3. Greta Garbo once claimed she never said, "I want to be alone." What did she insist she really said?

4. On the "Tonight" show, Johnny Carson suggested to this actor that he ought to pose *au naturel* in *Cosmopolitan* magazine.

5. Although legend has it that she was discovered in Schwab's Drugstore, the event actually occurred in Currie's Ice Cream Parlor, across the street from Hollywood High School. Who was she?

6. *The Adventures of Marco Polo* (1938) featured the exotic Sigrid Gurie, touted by Sam Goldwyn as The Norwegian Garbo. What surprising revelation helped to short-circuit her career?

7. According to this Tinsel Town myth, Howard Hughes designed a brassiere for this Hollywood newcomer, using aerodynamic principles.

8. Legend has it that this producer "discovered" Vivien Leigh just days before his much publicized search for the perfect Scarlett O'Hara ended.

9. It has been alleged that this legendary star appeared in two stag films, *The Casting Couch* and *Velvet Lips*.

10. According to biographer Charles Higham, this actress doesn't inhale on her Philip Morris cigarettes.

ANSWERS

# HOLLYWOOD MYTHS
## Don't Believe All You Hear

1  *The Lights of New York*, released in 1928.

2  MGM writer George Oppenheimer created the remark and won a contest among studio writers for coming up with a "Goldwynism" that would appear in print and be credited to their boss.

3  "I want to be *let* alone," which, as she pointed out, has a somewhat different meaning.

4  Carson's "spontaneous" suggestion to Burt Reynolds during a taping of the "Tonight" show was prearranged; the photo session had already taken place.

5  Lana Turner, then a student at Hollywood High, was first approached by Billy Wilkerson (editor of the *Hollywood Reporter*) in 1936, while drinking a Coke.

6  It was discovered that Sigrid was actually from Brooklyn, New York.

7  Jane Russell supposedly wore Hughes's brassiere, but cross-my-heart it was only so much Hollywood hype to promote the 1946 movie *The Outlaw*.

8  David O. Selznick was actually negotiating for the British star months before his search ended.

9  Joan Crawford. According to Hollywood folklore the star bought the films from a blackmailer for a hefty $100,000.

10  Bette Davis. During an interview with Davis he observed that she merely puffed on the forbidden weed.

BEHIND THE SCENES

# IT'S ALL DONE WITH MIRRORS

1. This star had his ears pinned to his head with spirit gum before he was allowed to face a camera.

2. A famous child star had ringlets affixed to her own hair to give her a full head of curls. Who was she?

3. Name the actress who disguised herself as "Lady Ainsley" so she could be given a screen test for the part of Elizabeth I in the movie *Mary of Scotland*.

4. Name the comedian who refused to have his nose fixed, but gave in to Sam Goldwyn's demand to bleach his hair blond.

5. Harpo took to stealing this star's wigs during takes of their Hollywood movies.

6. When he first arrived in Hollywood in 1924, Clark Gable had cosmetic dentistry to attend to this flaw.

7. Name the movie rock-and-roll idol who dyed his dark-blond locks black in the 1950s.

8. After filming *Saskatchewan* (1954), Shelley Winters complained about the inconvenience of standing in a ditch in order to kiss her leading man. Who was the diminutive actor?

9. When this Broadway actress came to Hollywood she was given a complete studio makeover before meeting Darryl F. Zanuck. When the movie mogul lunged for her, one of her falsies fell to the floor. Who was the well-padded actress?

10. When Kirk Douglas was first under contract to Paramount, makeup artists were instructed to fix this "flaw" in the actor's face. What was the offending facial feature?

ANSWERS
# IT'S ALL DONE WITH MIRRORS

1. Bing Crosby. When the hot lights melted the gum, his ears would pop back into place. He finally decided to leave his ears *au naturel* for filming.

2. Shirley Temple's additional curls were compliments of George Westmore.

3. When Ginger Rogers was first turned down for the part she employed a makeup artist to help her disguise herself for a screen test. Rogers confessed to her scheme and the part was given to Florence Eldridge.

4. Danny Kaye. After spotting Kaye in New York, Goldwyn wanted to make him a star despite Kaye's un-Hollywood-like appearance.

5. Margaret Dumont, the favorite target of Groucho's one-liners, was bald.

6. Gable had an unattractive gap between his front teeth.

7. Elvis Presley. Some speculate he dyed his hair to emulate his rock hero Roy Orbison.

8. Alan Ladd.

9. Judy Holliday, who quipped, "That's all right Mr. Zanuck, it's yours anyway."

10. The cleft in Douglas's chin. After they put putty in the offensive dimple, the actor looked like he had the world's widest chin.

BEHIND THE SCENES

# THE GOSSIPS
## Dishing and Digging

1. This trade paper was published weekly in New York until its debut as a Hollywood daily in 1933.

2. Although he wrote a popular newspaper column, this man was better known across the nation through his Sunday-evening radio broadcasts.

3. Afflicted with a crippling muscle disease as a child, she shocked her doctors and family by being feisty enough to form the first national fan club for singer Eddie Fisher at the age of fourteen. Who is this remarkable woman?

4. Columnist Joe Hyams made Hollywood history of sorts when *he* filed a $500,000 slander suit *against* a famous movie star. Who?

5. This columnist and radio-gossip-show host, who started out as a press agent, is also known for an infamous brawl with Errol Flynn.

6. This columnist, who started at the *New York Daily News* before moving to L.A. and the *Examiner*, often used Schwab's Drugstore as his office.

7. Louella Parsons once announced in her column that Sigmund Freud was being brought over from Europe as a technical adviser on the Bette Davis film *Dark Victory* (1939). Why did this prove to be an embarrassing "scoop"?

8. This Hollywood gossip magazine's article about Grace Kelly incited her father to show up at the magazine's office and throw a punch at the publisher.

9. This columnist became well-known as the mistress of F. Scott Fitzgerald.

10. In her book *The Whole Truth and Nothing But*, she claimed that Michael Wilding, Liz Taylor's fiancé, and Stewart Granger were having a homosexual relationship.

ANSWERS

# THE GOSSIPS
## Dishing and Digging

1   *Daily Variety*. It began because the weekly edition from New York was not timely enough to compete with the local *Hollywood Reporter*.

2   Walter Winchell.

3   Rona Barrett.

4   Cary Grant. The actor had publicly denied talking to Hyams after the writer published an interview with him. They settled out of court.

5   Jimmy Fidler. After the Flynn fight he always traveled with a bodyguard.

6   Sidney Skolsky.

7   At the time, Freud had been dead for several months.

8   *Confidential*, published by Robert Harrison in the mid-fifties, was sued for damages by a number of stars and made many out-of-court settlements, including one of $40,000 to Liberace.

9   Sheilah Graham.

10  Hedda Hopper. Ms. Hopper had to pay a hefty out-of-court settlement for that bit of Hollywood gossip and she also had to make a public apology to the parties involved.

BEHIND THE SCENES

# ROLE REVERSAL
## With a Cast of Thousands

1. George Raft as the lead, Otto Preminger as the villainous Nazi, and Lena Horne as the black entertainer were the original choices for roles in this classic 1942 film.

2. Mary Pickford declined the lead in this movie, saying it would destroy Hollywood's image forever.

3. F. Scott Fitzgerald's uncompleted final novel, *The Last Tycoon*, was made into a film in 1976. Name the movie about Fitzgerald that included scenes of him writing *The Last Tycoon*.

4. In 1951 Rudolph Valentino's life was made into a movie starring Anthony Dexter. Who starred in the 1977 version of *Valentino*?

5. Director Howard Hawks remade the rowdy film comedy *The Front Page* (1931) and the result was *His Girl Friday* (1940). What noteworthy change did Hawks create in the remake?

6. Hollywood is known for stretching the truth, but Greta Garbo had a right to be upset when they offered her the part of Rosalind Russell's mother in this 1947 film.

7. Name the rock star who was Barbra Streisand's first choice to play opposite her in the 1976 remake of *A Star is Born*.

8. In 1938 talent agent Sue Carol discovered this radio actor, who later became her husband and star of such movies as *This Gun for Hire* (1942) and *The Blue Dahlia* (1946). Who was he?

9. When Jack Warner offered the part of Henry Higgins in *My Fair Lady* (1964) to this actor, he said he wouldn't even see the film unless the part went to Rex Harrison.

10. She rejected the role of Mrs. Robinson, the middle-aged sexpot with a taste for young men played by Anne Bancroft in *The Graduate* (1967).

ANSWERS

# ROLE REVERSAL
## With a Cast of Thousands

1   *Casablanca*. The parts were of course filled by Humphrey Bogart, Conrad Veidt, and Dooley Wilson.

2   *Sunset Boulevard* (1950). Gloria Swanson, who accepted the lead, had no problem with Hollywood's image.

3   *Beloved Infidel* (1959), starring Gregory Peck and Deborah Kerr.

4   Ballet great Rudolph Nureyev. The film received less than mediocre reviews but is noteworthy for the creative casting of Huntz Hall as Jesse L. Lasky.

5   Hawks changed Hildy Johnson from a male to a female role. Rosalind Russell is the fast-talking newspaper reporter who can trade snappy dialogue with the best of them.

6   *Mourning Becomes Electra*. At the time Garbo was forty-two and "her daughter" Russell was forty.

7   Elvis Presley, who rejected the offer.

8   Alan Ladd. His marriage to Sue was the reverse of the traditional older man taking the inexperienced young actress under his wing. Seven years older than Ladd, Sue Carol managed his career and turned him into a box-office hit.

9   Cary Grant.

10  Doris Day's wholesome image could have been changed forever if she had accepted the role.

83

BEHIND THE SCENES

# ODD MAN OUT

1. Which of the following was *not* a member of the infamous Holmby Hills Rat Pack?
   a) Lauren Bacall.   b) Frank Sinatra.   c) Judy Garland.
   d) David Niven.   e) Spencer Tracy.

2. Unknown at age forty-two, he won the role that gave him instant stardom and created an entire new film genre—but he was not even invited to the film's West Coast premiere.

3. Which war movie did *not* star John Wayne?
   a) *Back to Bataan* (1944).   b) *They Were Expendable* (1945).
   c) *Sands of Iwo Jima* (1949).   d) *Halls of Montezuma* (1950).
   e) *Flying Leathernecks* (1951).

4. Why did Henry Fonda make no movies between 1949 and 1955?

5. The star of *The Invisible Man* (1933) made his movie debut in this film in which his face was never shown. He went on to many more-visible roles over the next twenty-two years. Who was he?

6. Lon Chaney, Jr. played almost all of the basic "monster-type" roles. Which of the following did he *not* play?
   a) The Wolf Man.   b) Frankenstein.   c) Dracula.
   d) The Mummy.   e) The Invisible Man.

7. Laurence Olivier tried to convince Sam Goldwyn to have his wife, Vivien Leigh, opposite him in this film classic. Instead Goldwyn cast Merle Oberon in the female lead. Name the film.

8. Rita Hayworth passed up the lead in this film comedy when she fell in love with Prince Ali Khan.

9. It is said that he ended William Haines's film career when the actor refused to end his relationship with Jimmy Shields.

10. Which one of these movies was *not* released in 1939?
    a) *Gone With the Wind.*   b) *The Wizard of Oz.*
    c) *Wuthering Heights.*   d) *Citizen Kane.*

ANSWERS
# ODD MAN OUT

1   Tracy was not a member of the social group Bogart described by saying: "We admire ourselves and don't care for anyone else."

2   Boris Karloff, uncredited on screen as The Monster in *Frankenstein* (1931), was at first considered so subordinate to the stars of the film (Colin Clive and Mae Clarke) that he was not asked to attend the premiere.

3   *Halls of Montezuma*, which starred Richard Widmark; all the others featured The Duke.

4   He returned to the Broadway stage during that period because he didn't like the movie roles he was being offered. He came back in 1955 to star in *Mr. Roberts*, the film version of a Broadway show he had starred in.

5   Claude Rains.

6   The Invisible Man. As for the others, he was in: *The Wolf Man* (1941), *The Ghost of Frankenstein* (1942), *Son of Dracula* (1943), and *The Mummy's Tomb* (1942) and *The Mummy's Ghost* (1944).

7   *Wuthering Heights* (1939). Had Goldwyn relented to Olivier's wishes, *Gone With the Wind* would have been minus Leigh as Scarlett O'Hara.

8   *Born Yesterday* (1950) was cast with Broadway actress Judy Holliday.

9   Louis B. Mayer, head of MGM, demanded Haines abandon his homosexual lover. Haines refused and took up a career as an interior decorator when he was blacklisted from the studio.

10  *Citizen Kane* (1941). Film buffs consider 1939 the greatest year in film history.

BEHIND THE SCENES

# RUMORS
## Maybe . . . and Maybe Not

1. After completing the filming of *The Man Who Loved Cat Dancing* (1973), this actor dropped out of sight for two months and rumors began circulating that he was dead.

2. Movie stars have been leaving their prints in the sidewalk outside Grauman's Chinese Theater since 1927, and there always seems to be room for more. What happens to the prints of stars that have faded over the years?

3. More than one source claims that this actress's "adopted" daughter is her child by actor Clark Gable.

4. Name the Hollywood director who died shortly after celebrating his forty-third birthday on William Randolph Hearst's yacht.

5. What was Louis B. Mayer's alleged method for controlling teenage Judy Garland's weight while she was under contract to MGM?

6. Name the child actor, star of *Skippy* (1931), who was accused by Walter Winchell in his column of being a midget.

7. According to James Bacon, studio head Harry Cohn hired thugs to threaten Sammy Davis, Jr. because he was romancing this Hollywood leading lady. The story goes he was ordered to drop the actress and marry a black woman.

8. Hollywood folklore has it that Louis B. Mayer ended this actor's career when the studio head ordered the sound engineers to distort deliberately the sound of the actor's voice in his first "talking" movie.

9. Rumor had it that this actor had a speech impediment and covered it up with his monosyllabic "yep" and "nope" conversations.

10. Name the sex star who was a master at the art of getting publicity and claimed to have an IQ of 164.

ANSWERS

# RUMORS
## Maybe . . . and Maybe Not

1. Burt Reynolds. He and co-star Sarah Miles had been implicated in the death of Miles's personal assistant David A. Whiting. The inquest ruled that Whiting's death was a suicide. The strain of the inquest took its toll on Reynolds, who suffered from exhaustion.

2. Rumor has it that the basement of the theater is filled with slabs of concrete containing the names of now-forgotten stars.

3. Loretta Young. Among her favorite charities is a Catholic home for unwed mothers.

4. Thomas Ince. The details of his death remain veiled in mystery. Some claim that Hearst shot the director in a jealous rage.

5. Mayer had a personal cook assigned to Judy Garland, who laced the star's food with Benzedrine (an appetite suppressant).

6. Jackie Cooper.

7. Kim Novak. Shortly after the alleged incident, Davis was married to a black nightclub performer named Loray White.

8. John Gilbert. The romantic star of silent films, his career ended when he whined through his talking movie debut, *His Glorious Night* (1929).

9. Gary Cooper may have talked that way in the movies, but in reality he was quite articulate.

10. Jayne Mansfield, who is better remembered for her bra size than her intelligence quotient.

BEHIND THE SCENES

# YOU OUGHT TO BE IN MOVIES

1. Babe Ruth played himself in what 1942 movie?

2. Former First Lady Pat Nixon made a brief appearance in what 1934 movie?

3. The film *Sincerely Yours* (1955) featured the movie debut of a TV star whom Warner Brothers was sure would be a big-screen success. Who?

4. In 1933, Paramount outbid the other studios and won the right to cast radio's biggest star in the leading role of *Hello Everybody*. Who was that star?

5. Ricky Nelson once co-starred (and sang) in what Howard Hawks western that starred John Wayne?

6. When William Randolph Hearst saw her screen test for MGM he broke down and cried, saying it was marvelous.

7. Author Truman Capote appeared in which Neil Simon movie?

8. His great-grandfather had been the leading Irish comedian at Drury Lane in London.

9. In the 1916 movie *My Official Wife*, filmed in New York, one of the extras hired was a famous revolutionary. Who was this well-known Russian?

10. Ted Turner, of Turner Broadcasting System Inc., purchased this studio for $1.5 billion in August 1985.

ANSWERS

# YOU OUGHT TO BE IN MOVIES

1. *Pride of the Yankees*, in which Gary Cooper played Ruth's teammate Lou Gehrig.

2. *Becky Sharp*.

3. Liberace. He did not make another movie until 1965.

4. Kate Smith. Although the film was a resounding box-office failure, Kate remained a gigantic star in radio and later on television.

5. *Rio Bravo* (1959). Ricky sang with Dean Martin and Walter Brennan.

6. Marion Davies, Hearst's paramour of thirty-four years.

7. *Murder by Death* (1976).

8. Tyrone Power.

9. Leon Trotsky, who was living in exile in the Big Apple. The Russian was renamed Mr. Brown on the studio poster and received five capitalistic dollars for his work.

10. Metro Goldwyn Mayer–United Artists. Turner bought the studio after an unsuccessful attempt to buy CBS, Inc.

BEHIND THE SCENES
# I WISH I'D SAID THAT

1. Who was Lillian Hellman talking about when she said, "You must realize that he regards himself as a nation"?

2. The immortal words, "I simply cannot eat on an empty stomach," were uttered by:
   a) Sydney Greenstreet.   b) Errol Flynn.   c) Orson Welles.
   d) John Barrymore.

3. Name the 1938 film that introduced the phrase, "Come with me to the Casbah."

4. Which actress popularized the expression, "Cigarette me, Big Boy?"

5. One of these is not a quote from a Will Rogers movie:
   a) "Advertising is where you make people believe that they must have something they've managed to do without all of their lives."
   b) "The American emblem shouldn't be an eagle but a can opener."
   c) "Chain stores are about as friendly as chain gangs."
   d) "When you rub elbows with the rich, the only thing you're guaranteed to get is shiny elbows."

6. Who said, "The only 'ism' in which Hollywood believes is plagiarism"?

7. Who said, "A brassiere is an unnecessary garment, actually unhealthy"?

8. When Mae West said, "C'mon up and see me sometime," who was she talking to?

9. What famous phrase is Warren Beatty credited with coining? (The phrase later became the title of a movie and hit song.)

10. Name the actor who said he was moving to Texas, "because the Texans will shoot communists on sight."

ANSWERS

# I WISH I'D SAID THAT

1. Samuel Goldwyn.

2. John Barrymore.

3. *Algiers*, starring Charles Boyer and Hedy Lamarr.

4. Ginger Rogers, in her first feature-length film, *The Young Man of Manhattan* (1930). She played a wisecracking flapper.

5. The "shiny elbows" quote is not from Rogers. All the rest are.

6. Dorothy Parker.

7. Jean Harlow. The actress personified the braless look in the thirties.

8. Cary Grant. Grant was an unknown actor on the Paramount lot when West spotted him. She insisted that he be in her movie *She Done Him Wrong* (1933).

9. "What's new, pussycat?" Producer Charlie Feldman overheard the actor using the come-on with the ladies. The 1965 film was scripted by Woody Allen.

10. Adolphe Menjou.

BEHIND THE SCENES

# CULT

1. In the 1950s, a popular location for science-fiction films was also used in the teen cult classic, *Rebel Without a Cause* (1955). What was it?

2. Drive-in movie critic Joe Bob Briggs reveres this movie, directed by Toby Hooper, as the undisputed "slice 'n' dice" drive-in cult favorite. What is it called?

3. The acclaimed master of the cheap horror/cheap western/cheap sci-fi cult film, this director is also known for giving a helping hand to newcomers, including Francis Ford Coppola, Peter Bogdanovich, Martin Scorsese, and Robert Towne.

4. James Dean was thrown out of what college fraternity on what campus?

5. Star of such turkeys as *The Well-Groomed Bride* (1946) and *Cat Women on the Moon* (1954), he is best known as the butt of wisecracks from Johnny Carson on the "Tonight" show.

6. This 1971 film about a May-December romance became a cult classic for a generation of college students.

7. What film opens with a discussion among Mary Shelley, Percy Shelley, and Lord Byron?

8. Faye Dunaway replaced this actress in the Joan Crawford role in *Mommie Dearest* (1981)

9. In 1969 *Playboy* magazine declared what actor to be the next decade's first cult hero.

10. This much maligned horror-comedy film featured a deadly vegetable-fruit as the star.

ANSWERS

# CULT

1 The Griffith Park Observatory, where James Dean and his high-school class went to see the planetarium show—and have a knife fight—was also often seen as a place where scientists worked frantically to save the earth, as in *When Worlds Collide* (1951).

2 *The Texas Chainsaw Massacre* (1974).

3 Roger Corman, whose illustrious credits include: *Attack of the Crab Monsters* (1957), *The Little Shop of Horrors* (1960), *The Wild Angels* (1966), and many, many more.

4 The Sigma Nu house at UCLA. Dean, ever the rebel, got into a fistfight with one of his fraternity brothers. He attended UCLA for one year before leaving to act in New York.

5 Sonny Tufts. His career was on the skids in the mid-fifties and he was arrested numerous times for public drunkenness.

6 *Harold and Maude*. The movie didn't turn a profit for twelve years. When Ruth Gordon finally received her $50,000 check for the project in 1983, she almost threw it away thinking it was a sweepstakes advertisement from *Reader's Digest*.

7 *Bride of Frankenstein* (1935). The episode was taken from real life. Poet Lord Byron held lively discussions in his Switzerland castle. One night, Byron's physician, Dr. Polidori, Percy and Mary Shelley, and Byron challenged each other to write the most horrifying story. The winner was Mary Wollstonecraft Shelley, who wrote *Frankenstein (or, the Modern Prometheus)*.

8 Anne Bancroft was replaced when she wasn't satisfied with any of the eighteen scripts written for the film.

9 Peter Fonda, whose role in *Easy Rider* (1969) as Captain America represented the quintessential antihero for a new generation.

10 *Attack of the Killer Tomatoes* (1978).

BEHIND THE SCENES

# TRUTH IS STRANGER . . .

1. The movie *Chinatown* (1974) tells the story of a scandal involving fictitious Los Angeles Water Commissioner Hollis Mulray. It was based on a famous L.A. water scam involving what real-life local official?

2. Steven Spielberg first wanted to make *E. T.* (1982) at this well-known Hollywood studio, but was refused, reputedly because he wanted 20 percent of the gross.

3. As a consequence of his 1950 marriage to Shirley Temple, Pacific Gas & Electric Company heir Charles Black was forced to make what great sacrifice?

4. While watching the rushes for the film *Hell's Angels* (1930), director Howard Hughes was upset with the airplane dogfighting sequences because the sky was cloudless. Why did the clear skies bother Hughes?

5. This was one of President Nixon's favorite movies, and he reputedly saw it one more time before announcing the 1970 invasion of Cambodia.

6. The 1976 remake of *A Star Is Born* was originally intended as a vehicle for what real-life husband and wife rock stars?

7. Screenwriter Ben Hecht had what unusual provision written into a contract in order to protect him from interference by Sam Goldwyn?

8. The 1951 film version of this Theodore Dreiser novel not only had a new cast of characters but also a new title, *A Place in the Sun*. What was the title of the book and earlier film version?

9. This well-known star of Hollywood horror films once played Jesus Christ on the Budapest stage.

10. Why did the 1979 Three Mile Island nuclear reactor incident have special meaning for film producer Michael Douglas?

ANSWERS

# TRUTH IS STRANGER...

1. The head of the Los Angeles Water Department, William Mulholland. Not surprisingly, the Mulholland Dam, which forms the Lake Hollywood reservoir, is named for him (as well as, of course, Mulholland Drive).

2. Walt Disney Studios turned down the extraterrestrial moneymaker.

3. He was dropped from the Social Register—for marrying an actress.

4. Because of the lack of clouds the airplanes had no counterpoint and thus appeared static. At great expense, Hughes had all the action shots refilmed.

5. *Patton* (1970).

6. James Taylor and Carly Simon. It is said that they did not do the movie because its story was a little too close to their own.

7. Hecht's arrangement stated that if Goldwyn spoke one word to him, the deal was off. After two weeks, Goldwyn made what he termed "purely a social call" to Hecht, and the writer canceled the deal—after being paid $10,000.

8. *An American Tragedy*, Dreiser's 1925 social commentary on American industrial life, was based on the actual killing of Grace Brown by Chester Gillette. Josef von Sternberg used the original book title for his 1931 film version.

9. Former stage actor Bela Lugosi. Following the First World War, Lugosi emigrated to Germany from his native Hungary. He eventually found his way onto a freighter bound for the United States.

10. The nuclear accident paralleled almost exactly the plot of the movie *The China Syndrome* (1979), which Douglas had been criticized for producing. The critics thought the film was too farfetched. Twelve days after the movie's release, the Three Mile Island accident occurred.

BEHIND THE SCENES

# GOOD SPORTS

1. While performing her own stunt in a movie, Katharine Hepburn contracted a virus that caused a weak tear duct, an impairment that still affects her to this day. How did it happen?

2. He barely escaped with his life when this actor insisted on doing his own stunt work for a scene in *Deliverance* (1972) that called for him to go over a waterfall on the Chattanooga River.

3. In his last film, *Escape from the Planet of the Apes* (1971), this onetime teenage idol played a monkey.

4. When President Johnson's daughter Lynda Bird married Charles Robb, she graciously invited this Hollywood actor to her wedding.

5. During the filming of this movie, an expert was hired to shoot a submachine gun inches from James Cagney.

6. In her movie scenes with Mickey Rooney, she had to stand in a hole so he would look taller.

7. According to Gary Cooper biographer Hector Arce, this actress fired a gun at Cooper when he went off on a five-week European holiday without her.

8. In 1965 heavyweight champion of the world Mohammed Ali claimed he knocked out Sonny Liston with a punch he learned from this actor.

9. While campaigning for Senator Eugene McCarthy for president in 1968, this actor consented to sign autographs for fans, something he didn't ordinarily do.

10. When Mike Todd was a kid in Minnesota he paid his friend Fat Libitsky to be the lookout for Todd's crap game. Who did Fat Libitsky grow up to become?

ANSWERS

# GOOD SPORTS

1. While making *Summertime* (1955) in Venice, Hepburn's role called for her to fall into a canal. She did and the water caused an infection.

2. Burt Reynolds convinced director John Boorman to let him take that dangerous "trip" after a professional stuntman declared the idea suicidal.

3. Sal Mineo.

4. George Hamilton, who had dated the President's offspring and escorted her to the Academy Awards.

5. *The Public Enemy* (1931). The camera caught the bullets hitting the building near Cagney's head.

6. Ann Rutherford, who played Rooney's girlfriend Polly in the Andy Hardy series.

7. Lupe Velez was the pistol-packing actress who gave Cooper the memorable send-off. Being a gentleman, Cooper never acknowledged the incident.

8. Stepin Fetchit. Fetchit said he learned the punch from boxer Jack Johnson.

9. Paul Newman. Rather than alienate potential McCarthy supporters, the actor agreed to sign autographs.

10. Comedian Jack E. Leonard.

BEHIND THE SCENES

# GOOD THINKING

1. In order to prepare for his first movie role, Brando moved into Birmingham's Veterans Hospital to live with paraplegic patients. Why?

2. Hollywood Boulevard between Sycamore and Gower, and Vine Street from Sunset to Yucca have the only sidewalks in Los Angeles that are cleaned six times a week. Why?

3. Before coming to Hollywood in 1934, the Hungarian-born Peter Lorre had his first English-speaking role in a British film directed by Alfred Hitchcock. What was strange about his being cast in the film?

4. Terry Hunt's club on La Cienaga Boulevard kept male and female patrons strictly segregated, yet was frequented by many Hollywood stars. Why?

5. What trick did Trocadero owner Billy Wilkerson use to get his nightclub off to a rousing start?

6. Bette Davis and John Garfield came up with an idea to support the servicemen in World War II that got virtually all of Hollywood involved. What was it?

7. Gangster Bugsy Siegel chose the Longden Tower Hill castle in Hollywood for an illegal gambling casino. What made the castle a perfect location for covert activities?

8. Name the Astaire and Rogers film whose title was altered under the Hollywood Production Code.

9. Name the community that was originally a bean field, then an unsuccessful oil field, and later a land development scheme designed to accommodate both the upper and middle classes.

10. In 1910 Hollywood's Board of Trustees banned *these* from their town.

ANSWERS

# GOOD THINKING

1. Brando's first movie, *The Men* (1950), deals with a paraplegic's relationship with his fiancée.

2. Those sidewalks represent the Walk of Fame. About eighteen hundred stars appear in the pavement to immortalize various Hollywood legends.

3. At the time Hitchcock interviewed him for the role, Lorre spoke no English. By nodding and smiling as the director spoke, he convinced Hitchcock that his English was adequate for the part of a villain in *The Man Who Knew Too Much* (1934).

4. Hunt's was one of the more popular health clubs in town. The facilities were used by Clark Gable, Marlene Dietrich, Ingrid Bergman, Cesar Romero, and others.

5. After large parties had packed the club its first three nights, people stopped coming. Wilkerson decided to put up the velvet rope outside and keep the band playing. Those who came to the door or phoned were told that the club was full and no reservations were available for the next two weeks. The Troc soon became one of Hollywood's most popular nightclubs of the thirties and forties.

6. The Hollywood Canteen, a converted barn that became a place where men and women in the armed forces could come and be entertained by the stars, as well as dance and chat with them.

7. The castle was on a hillside and had a bird's-eye view of any approaching police officers.

8. *The Gay Divorcee* (1934) was originally called *The Gay Divorce* and performed by Astaire on Broadway under the forbidden title.

9. Beverly Hills. Entrepreneurs Cook, Canfield, Green, and Whittier realized they could attract wealthy land investors if they had land available for middle-class shopkeepers and servants. The middle class could provide the services needed for the then-remote community of Beverly Hills.

10. Movie houses. The then-conservative town did not approve of the wicked movie industry.

BEHIND THE SCENES

# WHO SAID WHAT ABOUT WHOM?

One of the following personalities is being talked about in each of the following quotes. Match the subject with the quote: Gene Siskel, Greta Garbo, Elizabeth Taylor, Linda Blair, Sam Peckinpah, Jack Warner, Zsa Zsa Gabor, Bette Davis, Orson Welles, Clark Gable, Jane Fonda, John Belushi, Richard Burton, E. T., Doris Day.

1 "There, but for the grace of God, goes God."—Herman Mankiewicz.

2 "Let's just say that we don't double-date."—Roger Ebert.

3 "Oh, hell, I can kill five guys and have 'em buried in the time it takes him to kill one."—Howard Hawks

4 "At first I thought he was gushy, then I got used to him."—Drew Barrymore.

5 "I thought you were a fellow I know from Kansas City."—Groucho Marx.

6 "Who could take that scruffy, arrogant buffoon seriously?"—Eddie Fisher.

7 "Never fails to try and con my diamond rings from me."—Sammy Davis, Jr.

8 "He would rather make a bad joke than a good picture."—Jack Benny.

9 "An explosive little broad with a sharp left."—Jack Warner.

10 "I've been around so long, I knew her before she was a virgin."—Groucho Marx.

11 "I've known her since she was a French housewife."—Gore Vidal.

12 "A good man, but a bad boy."—Dan Aykroyd.

13 "When I was your age I was nineteen."—Victor Borge.

14 "He used to claim he was very dull in bed."—Eve Arden.

15 "Her face is inscrutable, but I can't vouch for the rest of her."—Oscar Levant.

100

ANSWERS

# WHO SAID WHAT ABOUT WHOM?

1   Orson Welles.

2   Gene Siskel.

3   Sam Peckinpah.

4   E. T.

5   Greta Garbo.

6   Richard Burton.

7   Elizabeth Taylor.

8   Jack Warner.

9   Bette Davis.

10  Doris Day.

11  Jane Fonda.

12  John Belushi.

13  Linda Blair.

14  Clark Gable.

15  Zsa Zsa Gabor.

# Legends

LEGENDS

# HUMPHREY BOGART

1. After he returned from his first unsuccessful try at Hollywood, how did Bogart support himself between stage roles in New York?

2. Why was Bogart afflicted with a lisp?

3. When Bogart was first summoned to Hollywood by Fox Films for what he thought was the lead role in a film called *The Man Who Came Back* (1930), he found that he had been hired for a totally different job. What was it?

4. Why did Humphrey Bogart name his motor launch Sluggy?

5. Bogart held court at lunchtime in this Beverly Hills restaurant almost every day when he was not working.

6. Bogart named his daughter Leslie in honor of fellow actor Leslie Howard. Why?

7. While under contract to Warner Brothers, Bogart was forced to play the role of Dr. Maurice Xavier in the only horror film of his career. What was its title?

8. Bogart and Raymond Massey each did their own stunt in one dangerous scene in *Action in the North Atlantic* (1943), which resulted in Massey's pants burning off and Bogie singeing his eyebrows. Why did they do it?

9. Agents Sam Jaffe and Mary Baker, who negotiated Bogart's contract with Warner Brothers, took out a $100,000 insurance policy on him during the making of *Casablanca* (1942). Why?

10. On May 21, 1945 Bogart married Lauren Bacall in:
    a) Their Holmby Hills home.   b) The galley of his yacht.
    c) Paris, France.   d) Ohio.

ANSWERS
# HUMPHREY BOGART

1  He was hired to play chess for one dollar a game in a Manhattan arcade.

2  It was the result of a poorly done operation on his lower lip to remove a splinter of wood that was embedded there in a childhood accident. The Warner Brothers publicity department later embellished this into a story of a shrapnel wound suffered in World War I combat.

3  He was assigned to be the voice coach to the actual lead, former silent-film actor Charles Farrell. Bogart eventually played bit parts in a few movies, and when his short contract expired and was not renewed, he returned to New York.

4  It was the same name he called his third wife, Mayo Methot. It derived from the many knock-down, drag-out fights that characterized their seven-year marriage.

5  Romanoff's.

6  After the two had been in the Broadway play *The Petrified Forest*, Howard insisted that Warner Brothers retain Bogart as his co-star in the 1936 film version or he would refuse his own starring role. The studio had wanted to replace Bogie with their contract star Edward G. Robinson.

7  *The Return of Dr. X* (1939).

8  The scene had called for the stars' doubles to leap from a ship into water that was aflame with oil. When Bogart taunted his co-star with the remark, "My double is braver than yours," they both ended up doing the stunt themselves.

9  Bogie's jealous wife Mayo Methot thought that he was in love with co-star Ingrid Bergman and threatened to kill him if he left her. Jaffe and Baker took her seriously.

10  At Malabar Farm, the home of friend Louis Bromfield, in Ohio.

LEGENDS

# MARLON BRANDO

1. Where was Marlon Brando born?
   a) Bangkok.  b) Calcutta.  c) Omaha.  d) Rangoon.

2. When agent Edith Van Cleve of MCA discovered Brando in 1944, he was performing in which Broadway play?

3. Name the comedian who was Brando's best friend from his early acting days in New York until the comedian's death in 1973.

4. Why did actress Anna Kashfi and Marlon Brando cancel their plans to be married in Arizona?

5. Brando was given this casting task for the remake of *Mutiny on the Bounty* (1962).

6. When he auditioned for this adaptation of a Broadway musical, Brando said of his own singing voice, "Sounds like the mating call of a yak." Which movie was he talking about?

7. Name the Puerto Rican actress who dated Brando on and off in the late fifties.

8. Brando hoped this movie would explore intelligently why young people form groups that seek expression in violence. Name the film.

9. Who was Sacheen Littlefeather?

10. Although he only worked on the film *Superman* for a total of twelve days, how much was Brando paid?
    a) $1 million.  b) $2 million.  c) $2.5 million.  d) $3 million.

ANSWERS

# MARLON BRANDO

1   Omaha, Nebraska. Early in his career Brando would fabricate stories about his upbringing, claiming to be born in various exotic places.

2   *I Remember Mama*. Brando played the unlikely role of Nels, son of Norwegian immigrants.

3   Wally Cox.

4   Kashfi was born in India and at that time Arizona banned interracial marriages.

5   Brando was to select a local Tahitian beauty to play Maimiti, Fletcher Christian's concubine. He chose Tarita Teriipaia, who some months later bore the actor a son, Tehotu.

6   *Guys and Dolls* (1955). The critics agreed.

7   Rita Moreno, who was a bit player in musicals and westerns when she and Brando met.

8   *The Wild Ones* (1954), the first of the motorcycle genre films. The movie did not live up to Brando's expectations.

9   An actress named Maria Cruz (she claimed to be an Apache princess), who made the nonacceptance speech when Brando declined the Academy Award for Best Actor in 1973, for his performance in *The Godfather*. The actor refused the Oscar because of America's treatment of the Indians.

10  For his portrayal of Jar-El, Superman's father from the planet Krypton, Brando was paid $2.5 million.

LEGENDS

# FRANK CAPRA

1. Frank Capra's educational background, although impressive, had little to do with the movies. What school did he graduate from, and for what profession was he trained?

2. Frank Capra once wrote gags for and later directed the films of what well-known silent-movie comedian?

3. How did Frank Capra support himself while in San Francisco in the early 1920s?

4. After the first preview audience hooted and laughed out of context at *Lost Horizon* (1937), what change did Frank Capra make to the movie to turn it into the huge success it eventually became?

5. In 1939 Capra, then president of the Screen Directors Guild, threatened the powerful Motion Picture Producers Association with a directors' strike and an embarrassing boycott of the upcoming Academy Awards presentations. Why?

6. Joseph P. Kennedy, then U.S. ambassador in London, sharply criticized one of Capra's films, saying it ridiculed democracy and that ". . . to show this film in foreign countries will do inestimable damage to American prestige all over the world." To what movie was he referring?

7. Between 1952 and 1956 Capra made four very successful nonfeature films entitled *Our Mr. Sun*, *Hemo the Magnificent*, *The Strange Case of the Cosmic Rays*, and *Meteora, the Unchained Goddess*. For what purpose did he make these films?

8. Why did Capra sue the Columbia studio to get out of his contract with them?

9. When Frank Capra was commissioned to produce the "Why We Fight" series of documentaries during World War II, he had no experience whatsoever in documentary filmmaking. What film did he see that led him to his brilliant approach to the project?

10. For which of the following did Frank Capra win the Academy Award as Best Director?
    a) *It Happened One Night* (1934).
    b) *Mr. Deeds Goes to Town* (1936).
    c) *You Can't Take It With You* (1938).
    d) *Mr. Smith Goes to Washington* (1939).
    e) *Arsenic and Old Lace* (1944).
    f) *It's a Wonderful Life* (1947).

ANSWERS

# FRANK CAPRA

1. He graduated from the California Institute of Technology in 1918 as a chemical engineer.

2. Harry Langdon, of the famous Mack Sennett studios. Capra also wrote gags for Our Gang comedies.

3. He earned his living playing draw poker, before getting a job as a prop man at a local movie company. He soon made his first film, *Fultah Fisher's Boarding House*, in San Francisco in 1924.

4. He threw out the first two reels, about twenty minutes, of the film and began the story at that point. This effectively changed the audience's perception of the entire movie—and made it a hit.

5. Capra was attempting to force the producers to recognize the guild as a bargaining agent, in the same way that the actors' and writers' guilds had already been accepted. The threat worked, and a major Hollywood "labor" victory was won.

6. *Mr. Smith Goes to Washington* (1939). Several U. S. senators also attacked the film, but three years later the movie was chosen by French theaters as the last English-language film to be shown before the Nazi-ordered ban on American and British films went into effect in occupied France.

7. They were educational scientific programs he made for an AT&T–sponsored television series. The shows first aired in 1956–57.

8. While in England, Capra found that Columbia had publicized a film there called *If Only You Could Cook* as a Capra picture, when in fact he had nothing to do with it. The suit was dismissed, but when it became apparent he would win a libel suit in London, Columbia chief Harry Cohn begged him to drop it and return to work, which he did.

9. The Nazi propaganda film *Triumph of the Will*. Capra found the movie so terrifying that he decided that the most powerful way to show the Nazi threat for what it was would be to use their own films against them. Nazi films, newsreels, and speeches were collected and edited into a powerful weapon for the U.S.

10. *Mr. Deeds Goes to Town*, *It Happened One Night*, and *You Can't Take It With You*; the latter two also won Oscars for Best Picture.

LEGENDS

# JOAN CRAWFORD

1. After Joan Crawford was married on October 8, 1928, she waited eight months before her in-laws condescended to meet her. Name her famous relatives.

2. Name the designer who created The Joan Crawford Look, using wide, padded shoulders.

3. According to her biographer Bob Thomas, Joan Crawford did not have a romantic interlude with which of the following men:
   a) Spencer Tracy.   b) Franchot Tone.   c) Clark Gable.
   d) Brian Donlevy.   e) William Paley.   f) Glenn Ford.

4. What was Joan Crawford's contribution to the American Women's Voluntary Services during World War II.

5. Though she was at home sick in bed with a temperature of 104 degrees F., Joan Crawford said, "It is the greatest moment of my life." Why?

6. Who was Lucille Fay LeSueur?

7. Joan Crawford once appeared in a television soap opera, "The Secret Storm," in 1968. What was the great actress doing on the boob tube?

8. In an interview with Bob Thomas in 1953, Joan Crawford severely criticized this female star for her shocking display of sexuality at the annual *Photoplay* magazine awards dinner. Who was she talking about?

9. Alfred Steele, chairman of the board of Pepsi Cola and Joan Crawford's fourth husband, helped the actress overcome a phobia she had had for years. What was the fear?

10. In her last film, *Trog* (1970), gossip had it that Crawford had a face-lift. What trick did hair stylist Ramon Guy use to smooth out the sixty-three-year-old actress's face?

ANSWERS

# JOAN CRAWFORD

1. Douglas Fairbanks and Mary Pickford, Hollywood's "royal" couple, did not think Joan was a proper wife for Douglas Fairbanks, Jr.

2. Gilbert Adrian, who accented the already broad shoulders with extra padding.

3. She had interludes with all of them.

4. Crawford helped to organize a day-care center for children of working women.

5. Joan had won the Academy Award for her performance in *Mildred Pierce* (1945). Crawford had not made a movie in two years and the award-winning performance was her comeback.

6. That is Joan Crawford's real name. Studio heads made her change it because they thought it sounded like LeSewer.

7. Joan graciously offered to fill in for her daughter, Christina, who was laid up in the hospital and unable to appear in her daily soap.

8. Marilyn Monroe, whose appearance in a skintight gold lamé gown caused a sensation.

9. Crawford was afraid of flying. After Steele's help she flew 98,000 miles in the first year and a half of their marriage.

10. Guy taped the sagging face and connected the tapes to rubber bands behind Crawford's head, and look, Ma, no more wrinkles!

LEGENDS

# BETTE DAVIS

1. Bette Davis created a fashion trend in the movie *Old Acquaintance* (1943). What was it?

2. The much-copied ritual from the film *Now, Voyager* (1942) in which Paul Henreid puts two cigarettes in his mouth, lights them both, and hands one to Bette Davis, actually came about out of frustration. What was the source of the frustration?

3. In the film *Summer of '42* (1971), what Bette Davis movie was playing at the Saturday matinee?

4. The Bette Davis movie *Marked Woman* (1937) was scheduled to be aired on CBS television in the sixties, but was pulled from the airwaves at the last minute. Why?

5. Why did the outcome of the 1948 presidential election have an effect on the Bette Davis movie *June Bride* (1948)?

6. He is buried on a hill overlooking Bette Davis's cottage, Butternut, in New Hampshire.

7. While she was performing on Broadway in 1953, he printed in his column that Bette Davis had cancer of the jaw. Who was the misinformed columnist?

8. Although the movie *Beyond the Forest* (1949) met with some of the worst reviews of Bette Davis's career, the movie did contain one of the actress's most famous lines of dialogue. What was it?

9. Name the gossip columnist who held the distinction of being the only member of the press who was banned from Bette Davis's movie sets.

10. While plugging her movie *Whatever Happened to Baby Jane?* (1962) on the Jack Paar show, a guest panelist did an imitation of Davis. Bette turned to the imitator and promptly told him to go to hell. Who was on the receiving end of Davis's wrath?

ANSWERS
# BETTE DAVIS

1. Davis appeared in a scene wearing a man's pajama top as a nightgown, which in essence was the first shorty nightgown.

2. The actors tried to copy an action from the Prouty best seller *Now, Voyager*, which involved handing lighted matches and cigarettes back and forth between Davis and Henreid. The matches kept going out, so Henreid invented the simplistic version of the romantic cigarette scene.

3. *Now, Voyager* (1942), which features the famous line, "Oh, Jerry, we have the stars, let's not ask for the moon."

4. The censors pulled the film because the "marked woman" was a prostitute who was brutalized by a gangster. CBS thought prostitution was too hot to handle on TV.

5. Filmed during the campaign, one line of dialogue had to be filmed twice. "How can I convert this McKinley stinker into a Dewey modern?" had to be reshot with Truman's name.

6. Ms. Davis's dog Tibby, who was her faithful pet for twelve years.

7. Walter Winchell. Davis was suffering from osteomyelitis.

8. "What a dump."

9. Sheilah Graham, who Davis thought treated her less than fairly in her columns.

10. Jonathan Winters.

LEGENDS

# WALT DISNEY

1. What special technique did Disney use to assure realistic-looking human characters in his animated films?

2. Who did the voice of Mickey Mouse in *Steamboat Willie* (1928), the animated star's first "talkie"?

3. Walt Disney produced which of the following World War II documentaries?
    a) *Victory Through Air Power.*   b) *Triumph of the Will.*
    c) *Inside Fascist Spain.*   d) *That Darned Nazi.*

4. Walt Disney makes an on-screen appearance (as himself) in which one of his feature films?

5. Walt Disney Studios' strange publicity stunt for the New York opening of *Pinocchio* (1940) turned out to be a major embarrassment. What happened?

6. Disney's *Darby O'Gill and the Little People* (1959) co-starred a young British actor who was to become a worldwide sensation in a role he would create just a few years later. Who?

7. How did Walt Disney discover Fess Parker for the role of *Davy Crockett* (1955)?

8. Which of the following did *not* star perennial Disney leading lady Hayley Mills?
    a) *Pollyanna* (1960).   b) *The Parent Trap* (1961).
    c) *In Search of the Castaways* (1962).   d) *The Incredible Journey* (1963).
    e) *That Darn Cat!* (1965).   f) *The Moon-Spinners* (1964).

9. This most commercially and critically successful of all the Disney films earned thirteen Academy Award nominations and won five of them.

10. The Disney Studios co-produced a 1980 release that, ironically, was about a character who had been a longtime Disney rival. Who?

## ANSWERS
# WALT DISNEY

1. He would first shoot a live-action version of the cartoon scenes, using real actors. His illustrators could then study the movement of the actors when doing the animation.

2. Walt Disney originally did the voice for his cartoon creation.

3. *Victory Through Air Power*, which used animation to demonstrate the importance of the long-range bomber (1943).

4. *The Reluctant Dragon* (1941), which was actually a behind-the-scenes look at the Disney Studios that included a making of the twelve-minute cartoon to which the title refers.

5. Eleven midgets were hired to dress up as Pinocchio and cavort about on the theater marquee. Unfortunately, after some liquor at lunchtime, the midgets became rowdy—and naked—and had to be removed by police.

6. Sean Connery, who was still three years away from his first James Bond 007 role in *Dr. No* (1962).

7. Some Disney people were screening the science-fiction movie *Them* (1954) (about giant ants) and noticed Parker in a brief but impressive scene.

8. *The Incredible Journey* (1963) starred a cat and two dogs trekking across Canada. Hayley was making *Summer Magic* (1963) at the time.

9. *Mary Poppins* (1964). Julie Andrews won one of those Oscars as Best Actress.

10. *Popeye* (1980). Disney Studios contributed financially and with some post-production technical work to the feature film about this cartoon rival of fifty years.

LEGENDS

# CLARK GABLE

1. What was Clark Gable's real name?
   a) Chris Cross.   b) William Gable.   c) Douglas Wainsworth.   d) Tom Graver.

2. Gable's first two wives had something in common. What was it?

3. In 1934 he was selected for a role in this film. Gable told director Capra he'd give the movie a try, but if after a few days Capra didn't like Gable's performance he would call the whole thing off. What was the movie?

4. Name the thirteen-year-old singer who sang "You Made Me Love You" at Gable's thirty-sixth birthday party.

5. Who was the first choice for the part of Rhett Butler in *Gone With the Wind* (1939)?

6. When he first dated this actress in 1936, and invited her up to his apartment for a drink, she wisecracked, "Who do you think you are, Clark Gable?" Who was the witty actress?

7. In the summer of 1942 Clark Gable did something to honor his late wife Carole Lombard's request. What was it?

8. In 1957 what special tribute was Gable given by Congress on his twenty-fifth anniversary in films?

9. Gable died November 16, 1960, just after this film was completed.

10. After Clark Gable's death, what significant event took place on March 20, 1961, at 7:10 A.M.?

ANSWERS

# CLARK GABLE

1. William Clark Gable, born February 1, 1901, in Cadiz, Ohio. Gable's father's name was changed from Goebel.

2. Both Josephine Dillion and Ria Langhan were years older than Gable, Dillion by fourteen years and Langham by seventeen.

3. *It Happened One Night* (1934), which won Oscars not only for Gable and co-star Claudette Colbert, but also for director Capra and screenwriter Robert Riskin. It also won the coveted Best Picture Award.

4. Judy Garland. Special lyrics for the song were written for the event. Judy made a recording of this unique version of the song in 1938.

5. Gary Cooper, who at the time had just signed a contract with Goldwyn Studios. Luckily for Gable, Goldwyn was unwilling to loan Cooper out to MGM.

6. Carole Lombard, who was later to become Mrs. Clark Gable.

7. Gable enlisted in the army. Carole Lombard had been killed earlier that year in a plane crash returning from a tour selling war bonds. Lombard had urged Gable to join the army.

8. Rep. Wayne L. Hays, Democrat of Ohio, read a tribute to The King that is part of the *Congressional Record*.

9. *The Misfits* (1961). Co-star Marilyn Monroe shared a sad coincidence with Gable. It was to be the last screen appearance for both of them.

10. Gable's only child, John Clark Gable, was born.

LEGENDS

# GONE WITH THE WIND

1. Peggy Marsh of Atlanta described the story of *Gone With the Wind* as "... just a simple story of some people who went up and some who went down, those who could take it and those who couldn't." What did she have to do with the picture?

2. Clark Gable was originally reluctant to play Rhett Butler because he feared the role was "too big an order" for him. What eventually convinced him to take it?

3. Which of the following did *not* test for the part of Scarlett O'Hara?
    a) Katharine Hepburn.   b) Loretta Young.   c) Lana Turner.
    d) Tallulah Bankhead.   e) Helen Hayes.

4. The movies *King Kong* (1933), *The Last of the Mohicans* (1936), and *Little Lord Fauntleroy* (1936) all contributed in a unique way to one famous scene in GWTW. How?

5. At one point, David O. Selznick had decided that Paulette Goddard had won the role of Scarlett O'Hara. Why was he forced to change his mind?

6. The scene in which Scarlett makes her way through hundreds of wounded Confederate soldiers at the Atlanta railroad station required 2,500 extras to play soldiers, but the Screen Extras Guild had only 1,500 available. How was this problem solved?

7. Susan Myrick, known as the Emily Post of the South, contributed what valuable service to the making of GWTW?

8. Approximately what percentage of the footage shot was actually used on screen in GWTW?
    a) 5 percent.   b) 15 percent.   c) 25 percent.   d) 50 percent.
    e) 66 percent.

9. Which of the following did *not* direct any of GWTW?
    a) George Cukor.   b) Victor Fleming.   c) Sam Wood.
    d) William Wyler.

10. *Gone With the Wind* premiered on December 15, 1939, in Atlanta. By the end of its run, in June 1940, approximately how many people had paid admission to see it?
    a) 1 million.   b) 10 million.   c) 25 million.   d) 100 million.

ANSWERS

# GONE WITH THE WIND

1. Marsh (her married name), who was born Margaret Mitchell, wrote the novel on which the film was based.

2. Money . . . and love. Gable wished to divorce his wife Rhea so he could marry Carole Lombard. Faced with the prospect of paying an exorbitant divorce settlement, he could not afford to turn down the part.

3. Tallulah Bankhead. Even Lucille Ball got to *read* for it.

4. The sets from these films were among those repainted and torched in the "burning of Atlanta" scene.

5. Goddard was openly living with Charlie Chaplin, who was already becoming a controversial figure, and it was not certain whether they were actually married. The public was so morally indignant about her private life that Selznick could not risk casting her in the starring role.

6. Producer David O. Selznick ordered one thousand dummies mixed in with the real bodies, and insisted that this be kept secret.

7. She was one of several experts hired to advise on southern dialect and manners.

8. Only 5 percent. Though 449,512 feet of film were shot, just 20,300 feet made it to the screen, a ratio of about 20 to 1.

9. William Wyler. Cukor started the picture and was soon fired and replaced by Fleming, who quit and was replaced by Wood, who later shared the duties with Fleming when the latter returned to the film.

10. Some 25 million people. Considering that the entire population of the United States at the time was just 132 million, this was quite a figure.

LEGENDS

# CARY GRANT

1. In 1922 Cary Grant worked at Coney Island. What was his job?

2. This leading lady said of her soon-to-be leading man, "If this one can talk, I'll take him."

3. Everyone knows that Cary Grant's real name is Archibald Leach, but can you name the film in which Archibald Leach's name is carved on a tombstone?

4. Name the Hollywood actor that shared Cary Grant's bachelor pad on and off for almost ten years.

5. Grant first met her during the filming of *The Pride and the Passion* (1957) and although married to Betsy Drake at the time, he proposed marriage.

6. Why did Betsy Drake send Grant a telegram in July 1956 that ended with, "Your safe, sound and rescued wife"?

7. The day after his marriage to her on July 3, 1942, Cary Grant went back to the movie set of *Once Upon a Honeymoon* (1942). Who was the bride who didn't have a honeymoon?

8. Grant brought a $10 million lawsuit against comedian Chevy Chase in October 1980. Why?

9. Name the magazine that sent a telegram to Cary Grant asking, "How Old Cary Grant?" to which Grant replied, "Old Cary Fine, How You?"

10. For what movie did Cary Grant win his Academy Award in 1970?

ANSWERS

# CARY GRANT

1. Grant walked on stilts in costume to advertise the amusement park.

2. Mae West, who chose the then unknown Grant for her leading man in *She Done Him Wrong* (1933).

3. *Arsenic and Old Lace* (1944). The screwball comedy took place at the Brewster home, which was right in the middle of a Brooklyn cemetery.

4. Randolph Scott. Even when Scott married his childhood friend Mariana du Pont, Grant and Scott continued to share the same house.

5. Sophia Loren. The Italian actress resisted Grant's charm and married Carlo Ponti during the making of another film starring Cary Grant, *Houseboat* (1958).

6. Drake had been a passenger on the ill-fated ship *Andrea Doria*, the night it collided with the *Stockholm*.

7. Barbara Hutton, the Woolworth heiress.

8. Grant sued Chase for slander. On the television show "Tomorrow," Chase commented on Grant's sexuality by saying, "What a gal."

9. According to Grant's biography by Geoffrey Wansell, *Haunted Idol*, the frequently quoted incident never occurred.

10. Unbelievably, Grant never won an Oscar for a movie role, but the Academy honored him with a special honorary Oscar.

LEGENDS

# KATHARINE HEPBURN

1. Katharine Hepburn's father's profession was:
    a) Shakespearean actor.   b) Urologist.   c) Gym instructor.
    d) Wheat farmer.

2. At the age of eleven, a personal tragedy touched Katharine Hepburn's life. What was it?

3. Yes, Katharine Hepburn was married once, but who was the lucky fella?

4. While filming *A Bill of Divorcement* (1932), John Barrymore tried to seduce the young Katharine Hepburn by inviting her into his dressing room and flinging off all his clothes. How did Hepburn respond?

5. In 1933 Kate Hepburn appeared in a disastrous production on Broadway called *The Lake*. Her performance inspired an often-quoted line from Dorothy Parker. What was Ms. Parker's reaction to Hepburn?

6. What physical "flaw" makes Katharine Hepburn the most self-conscious?

7. One of Katharine Hepburn's most unusual co-stars was named Nissa. Who was Nissa?

8. Why does Katharine Hepburn refuse to eat in restaurants?

9. In 1962 her relationship with this actor was revealed for the first time in a *Look* magazine article by Bill Davidson.

10. Hepburn's interview on this television show in 1973 was a first for the legendary actress.

ANSWERS

# KATHARINE HEPBURN

1. Dr. Thomas Norval Hepburn, a urologist, was a pioneer in the study of sexual hygiene.

2. Kate found her older brother Tom hanging dead in the attic. The reasons for his untimely death have never been discovered.

3. Ludlow Ogden Smith. They were married secretly in 1928 in Hartford, Connecticut. The marriage was too much for the independent actress and they separated after three weeks.

4. Terrified, Hepburn told Barrymore, "My father doesn't want me to make babies."

5. "She ran the gamut of emotions from A to B."

6. Her long neck, which she often covers with scarves and high collars. In her films, she is lit with a small spotlight to de-emphasize her neck.

7. Nissa was the leopard in the movie *Bringing Up Baby* (1938).

8. The actress claims she passes out in restaurants. The reclusive Hepburn gets nervous when people are watching her eat and it makes her ill and faint.

9. Spencer Tracy. Although she and Tracy had been romantically involved for years it had never been announced publicly.

10. "The Dick Cavett Show." She was so enchanting on the program that she was flooded with offers of work.

LEGENDS

# ALFRED HITCHCOCK

1. Hitchcock got his first job in the movies in 1920. What was it?

2. Why did Hitchcock make cameo appearances in his films?

3. What unusual filming method did Alfred Hitchcock use for the making of *Rope* (1948)?

4. Hitchcock had artist Salvador Dali collaborate with him to design what surreal sequence in one of his films?

5. What did Carole Lombard do in response to Hitchcock's infamous statement that "all actors are cattle"?

6. Which of the following is a MacGuffin?
    a) The assassination attempt in *The Man Who Knew Too Much* (1956).
    b) The secret formula in *The 39 Steps* (1935).
    c) The tune to be remembered in *The Lady Vanishes* (1938).
    d) The hidden uranium in *Notorious* (1946).

7. Hitchcock's economical technique of "editing in the camera," that is, shooting only those camera angles that he planned to use in the final edited film, greatly angered the producer of his first American film. Why?

8. Hitchcock's four-time leading man Jimmy Stewart has often been described as the director's "alter ego," playing characters for him that have personified Hitchcock's own quirks and attitudes. What actor is said to have played the idealized man Hitchcock *wished* he himself could be?

9. Alfred Hitchcock was known to be fascinated with the cool blond beauties he always starred in his films, but is alleged to have actually made an overt sexual proposition to only one leading lady. Who?

10. Which of the following won Hitchcock an Academy Award for Best Director:
    a) *Rebecca* (1940).   b) *Lifeboat* (1944).   c) *Spellbound* (1945).
    d) *Rear Window* (1954).   e) *Psycho* (1960).

ANSWERS
# ALFRED HITCHCOCK

1   In those days, the captions that provided the dialogue and narrative for silent films also contained little illustrations. Hitchcock provided these title designs for the London studio of Paramount's Famous Players-Lasky.

2   He did it first in *The Lodger* (1927) out of simple necessity; as he put it, "We had to fill the screen." He continued doing it out of superstition, and finally as a joke for his audiences.

3   The film was shot as a series of single camera, uninterrupted, ten-minute takes: there are no cuts to different scenes, only continuous action from one roving point of view. The technique was never tried again.

4   The dream sequence in *Spellbound* (1945). Hitchcock said he wanted Dali because he thought the artist could bring the required "visual sharpness and clarity" to the scene.

5   On the first day on the set of *Mr. and Mrs. Smith* (1941), Hitchcock arrived to find that his leading lady had set up a corral containing three cows, each with the name of one of the film's stars around its neck.

6   All of the above. Each was a MacGuffin, something Hitchcock described as neither relevant nor important to the plot, but that starts and keeps the story in motion.

7   David O. Selznick, producer of *Rebecca* (1940), was enraged because Hitchcock effectively took away Selznick's power to control the final editing of the movie, something the producer had always considered to be his privilege.

8   Cary Grant, ever suave in his four Hitchcock films, supposedly personified all that the director wanted to be.

9   Tippi Hedren, who starred in *The Birds* (1963) and *Marnie* (1964). She refused his advance and consequently did not work with him again.

10  None. Although nominated for the five films above, he never won the Oscar. In 1968 he was given the Academy's career consolation prize, the Irving Thalberg Award for "consistent high level of production achievement."

LEGENDS

# MARILYN MONROE

1. Marilyn Monroe had what parts of her anatomy remodeled at age twenty-three?

2. Which of the following was *not* alleged to have had an affair with Marilyn Monroe?
    a) Frank Sinatra.   b) Tony Curtis.   c) Marlon Brando.
    d) Yves Montand.   e) Harry Cohn.

3. Columnist Ed Sullivan described a musical number in one of Marilyn's films as ". . . easily one of the most flagrant violations of good taste this observer has ever witnessed." What was he describing?

4. Why were Marilyn Monroe's drama coaches Natasha Lytess and, later, Paula Strasberg, so dreaded by the directors of her movies?

5. Marilyn Monroe's long delays in getting ready between each take of a scene were legendary. What trick did director Joshua Logan use to prevent her from losing concentration?

6. The filming of Marilyn's famous scene in *The Seven Year Itch* (1955), in which her skirt is blown up above her waist while she stands over a subway grating, helped bring about what traumatic event in her personal life?

7. At Madison Square Garden in May 1962, Peter Lawford introduced her as "the late Marilyn Monroe," making a joke of her legendary tardiness. What was the event?

8. In 1961 Marilyn was picked to star as Sadie Thompson in a television adaptation of Somerset Maugham's *Rain*, but backed out. Why?

9. Of a world-famous figure, Marilyn reportedly said: "Give me two days alone with him and, of course, he'll want to marry me." Who was she talking about?

10. Marilyn Monroe and Arthur Miller worked together on only one film project. Name the movie.

ANSWERS

# MARILYN MONROE

1. Her jaw was redone and the tip of her nose was bobbed.

2. Tony Curtis. He in fact detested working with her on *Some Like It Hot* (1959).

3. Marilyn's "Tropical Heat Wave" number in *There's No Business Like Show Business* (1954). With each leg kick it appeared that she was wearing no underwear.

4. Because Marilyn insisted on having her drama coach on the set, and would not consider a scene good enough to be a final take unless the coach approved, regardless of what the film's director said.

5. While making *Bus Stop* (1956), Logan did not call "cut" to end a take but kept the cameras rolling, repositioned Marilyn as she was at the beginning of the scene, and quietly told her to "go ahead" again.

6. Her divorce from Joe DiMaggio. He was outraged by the scene and they announced their divorce two weeks later.

7. President John F. Kennedy's birthday party. Ms. Monroe sang "Happy Birthday" to the President.

8. NBC refused to use her acting teacher Lee Strasberg as director because he had no television experience. Marilyn would not do it with any other director.

9. Prince Rainier of Monaco, who married another Hollywood star, Grace Kelly.

10. *The Misfits* (1961), Marilyn's last film, which also marked the final screen appearance of Clark Gable.

LEGENDS

# JAMES STEWART

1. As a young actor in New York, Jimmy Stewart shared an apartment with what other struggling beginner?

2. What well-known columnist claimed to be responsible for bringing Jimmy Stewart to the attention of Hollywood?

3. When Jimmy Stewart was a young man, he was known to take his favorite musical instrument everywhere and play it with very little coaxing. What was it?

4. What did the following Jimmy Stewart characters all have in common: Rupert Cadel, L. B. Jeffries, Ben McKenna, Scottie Ferguson?

5. What type of unique competition was held at a New York theater in conjunction with the opening of Jimmy Stewart's film *You Can't Take It With You* (1938)?

6. For which film did Stewart win an Academy Award for Best Actor:
    a) *Mr. Smith Goes to Washington* (1939).
    b) *The Philadelphia Story* (1940).
    c) *It's a Wonderful Life* (1946).
    d) *Harvey* (1950).
    e) *Anatomy of a Murder* (1959).

7. What major military decoration did Jimmy Stewart receive from the air force for service in World War II?

8. Which of the following are *not* known to have dated Jimmy Stewart:
    a) Jean Harlow.  b) Ginger Rogers.  c) Lana Turner.
    d) Marlene Dietrich.  e) Bette Davis.

9. When Jimmy Stewart won the role of Monty Stratton in *The Stratton Story* (1949), he beat out what friend and well-known actor who badly wanted the part?

10. In 1972 Jimmy Stewart received an honor for his eighteen western roles, but it did not come from Hollywood. What was it?

ANSWERS

# JAMES STEWART

1. Henry Fonda roomed with Stewart in a flat on Sixty-fourth Street off Central Park West.

2. Hedda Hopper introduced him to a studio talent scout when Stewart was a stage actor on the East Coast, but nothing came of his screen test. Several months later, however, an MGM scout who had seen Stewart in several shows finally brought him to Hollywood.

3. An accordian.

4. They represent his four starring roles for Alfred Hitchcock in, respectively, *Rope* (1948), *Rear Window* (1954), *The Man Who Knew Too Much* (1956), and *Vertigo* (1958).

5. A Jimmy Stewart Sound-Alike Contest was held at Brooklyn's Loew's Pitkin theater. It was won by an unemployed plumber who imitated Stewart on a basketball court.

6. *The Philadelphia Story*. He was nominated for all of the above.

7. After leading his bomber squadron on a particularly hazardous mission over Germany, Maj. James Stewart was awarded the Distinguished Flying Cross. He also received the Air Medal, the croix de guerre, and seven battle stars.

8. Only Bette Davis. Until his marriage at age forty-one, Stewart had long been considered the most eligible bachelor in Hollywood.

9. Ronald Reagan, who said, "When Jimmy landed the part, I was so disappointed, I began thinking of other fields." The rest is history.

10. He was elected to the Cowboy Hall of Fame, a privilege generally granted only to *real* cowboys.

LEGENDS

# ELIZABETH TAYLOR

1. Liz Taylor was almost rejected for what role because she was too short?

2. Who was seventeen-year-old Elizabeth Taylor's first "real" boyfriend?

3. How did Liz Taylor force MGM to give a contract to British actor Michael Wilding?

4. The actor whom Liz Taylor described as her "dearest, most devoted friend" remained her close friend until his untimely death. Who?

5. While Liz Taylor was married to Eddie Fisher—and before she met Richard Burton—she and a certain Ph.D. more than thirty years her senior began an affair that lasted for a few years. Who was he?

6. Which of these unlikely personalities was alleged to have had a secret affair with Elizabeth Taylor:
   a) Andy Warhol.   b) Ingemar Johansson.   c) J. Edgar Hoover.
   d) Joan Crawford.   e) Elvis Presley.

7. After the scandalous shenanigans of Liz Taylor and Richard Burton helped to contribute to the financial disaster of *Cleopatra* (1963), how did Twentieth Century-Fox retaliate against the two stars?

8. In 1963 Elizabeth Taylor became the highest salaried television performer ever to do a single one-hour show. What did she do?

9. When did Elizabeth Taylor make her first appearance in a Broadway play?

10. Elizabeth Taylor claims that this was the only time she had ever shared a room with a woman.

ANSWERS
# ELIZABETH TAYLOR

1. Velvet Brown in *National Velvet* (1944). Producer Pandro S. Berman eventually decided to wait a few months for the eleven-year-old Liz to grow.

2. Football star Glenn Davis. The two were to be engaged, but it was called off after Liz met millionaire Bill Pawley—and became engaged to him instead.

3. She told MGM that Wilding, whom she intended to make her second husband, could not afford to leave his film career in England to marry her, so she was going to leave the studio to live with him in his country. MGM quickly came up with an excellent contract offer for Wilding.

4. Montgomery Clift, who met Liz when they were in *A Place in the Sun* (1951), and kept up their friendship until he died in 1966.

5. Syndicated political columnist Max Lerner.

6. According to biographer Kitty Kelley, former heavyweight boxing champ Ingemar Johansson sparred with Liz. Kelley quotes Max Lerner, another Liz affair, on this match.

7. The studio sued them for $50 million, claiming that their misconduct had destroyed the film.

8. CBS's "Elizabeth Taylor in London." She conducted a tour of famous British locales and was paid $500,000.

9. In 1981, at age forty-nine, she appeared on Broadway in a revival of Lillian Hellman's *The Little Foxes*.

10. Taylor was referring to her stay at the Betty Ford Center for treatment of her alcoholism.

LEGENDS

# JOHN WAYNE

1. The young Marion Morrison (John Wayne) was able to go to the movies as often as five times a week. How was he able to afford such a luxury?

2. After graduating from Glendale Union High School, Wayne was very disappointed he was not accepted to this institution of higher learning.

3. Republic Pictures cast Wayne in *Singing Sandy* (1935), in which the Duke strummed a guitar and sang a few off-key numbers to his horse. Who replaced Wayne as the singing cowboy?

4. *Stagecoach* (1939), directed by John Ford, was Wayne's first big commercial success. What personal tragedy marred the picture for Wayne?

5. The movie that John Wayne first starred in, *The Big Trail* (1929), was filmed using a revolutionary technique. What was it?

6. In court she accused Wayne of throwing a bottle of rubbing alcohol at her, punching her in the nose, and calling her names. Who was she?

7. The Waynes' family dog, Blackie, once had his picture in the newspapers for being a hero. Why?

8. According to his daughter Melinda Wayne, the Duke used this form of punishment on his children.

9. At the Republican National Convention in 1952, which candidate did Wayne support?

10. What was the vice that finally killed John Wayne?

ANSWERS
# JOHN WAYNE

1. Wayne's father's pharmacy in Glendale, California, was in the same building as a movie theater. The theater owner let the young Morrison in for free.

2. The United States Naval Academy. He did, however, receive a scholarship to the University of Southern California.

3. Gene Autry.

4. Wayne's father, Clyde Morrison, died just before work on the movie started.

5. It was called 70mm Grandeur (the precursor to CinemaScope). Unfortunately the film opened just after the Wall Street crash and movie theaters were unable to buy the needed equipment to show the film. A 35mm version was released.

6. Esperanza Bauer Wayne, the second Mrs. John Wayne. The Duke countered her vicious attacks and the judge called it a draw.

7. At 3:00 A.M. on January 14, 1958, Blackie's barks woke the sleeping Mrs. Wayne, who fled with her infant daugher Aissa when she realized the house was on fire. The Duke was on location in Tokyo at the time.

8. The silent treatment. He wouldn't talk to them.

9. Sen. Joseph McCarthy. Wayne is quoted as having said, "They say I'm a right-winger, but I consider myself a liberal."

10. Wayne, who died of lung cancer in 1979, smoked five packs of unfiltered cigarettes a day.

LEGENDS

# THE WIZARD OF OZ

1. Assistant producer Arthur Freed is credited with convincing MGM exec Louis B. Mayer to change his mind about removing a particular scene from *The Wizard of Oz*. What scene was it?

2. Ray Bolger (Scarecrow), Bert Lahr (Lion), and Jack Haley (Tin Man) were not allowed to eat in the studio commissary while working on the picture. Why?

3. Which of the following worked at one time or another as director of the film?
    a) Richard Thorpe.   b) George Cukor.   c) Victor Fleming.
    d) King Vidor.   e) Frank Capra.

4. Margaret Hamilton, the Wicked Witch, was involved in a frightening accident on the set during shooting. What happened?

5. There were 124 midgets hired to play munchkins and almost as many stories about their antics. Which of the following is *not* alleged to have happened:
    a) One midget bit the leg of an MGM policeman who was barring his way.
    b) A female midget propositioned a stagehand.
    c) A midget fell into a studio toilet and was trapped there until somebody found him.
    d) Halfway through the film, several midgets left to join a traveling circus.

6. At only $125 per week, she was the lowest paid of all the major characters in the movie.

7. How was the Wicked Witch "melted" in the end?

8. The seedy coat worn by Professor Marvel (in the Kansas sequence) was picked up by the wardrobe department in a Hollywood secondhand store. Who was the previous owner whose name was discovered sewn inside a pocket?

9. Originally selected to play the Scarecrow role, he was switched to the Tin Man and then dropped altogether when he became ill from his aluminum-dust makeup.

10. Match the prop with the price it brought at the MGM auction:
    Dorothy's ruby slippers.           $450.
    The Wicked Witch's Hat.            $1,000.
    The Wizard's suit.                 $2,400.
    The Cowardly Lion's costume.       $650.
    Dorothy's gingham dress.           $15,000.

ANSWERS

# THE WIZARD OF OZ

1. The one in which Judy Garland sings "Over the Rainbow." Mayer had demanded the scene be cut after seeing the first sneak preview.

2. The sight of their made-up faces, covered with rubber, fur, and aluminum paste, was too disgusting for their fellow diners. The studio agreed to pay for their lunches if the trio would eat in their dressing rooms.

3. Richard Thorpe worked twelve days, George Cukor worked three days, Victor Fleming was the credited director, and King Vidor added finishing touches. Frank Capra had nothing to do with *The Wizard of Oz*.

4. She caught on fire. When the witch disappeared in a puff of smoke and fire after her first appearance in Munchkinland, the flames caught her broom, severely burning Hamilton's face and hands.

5. At no point during filming did any midgets leave to join a traveling circus.

6. Terry, the female Cairn terrier who played Dorothy's dog, Toto. Terry's owner-trainer, Carl Spitz, was the first trainer to teach movie animals to respond to silent commands.

7. She stood on a hydraulic platform that was lowered into the floor of the stage while her costume, with dry ice inside it to create the vapors, remained fastened to the floor.

8. L. Frank Baum, author of *The Wizard of Oz*. Dubious as it may seem, Baum's widow allegedly verified that the coat had indeed belonged to her husband.

9. Buddy Ebsen, who went on to become a TV star in "The Beverly Hillbillies" and "Barnaby Jones."

10. Dorothy's ruby slippers, $15,000; The Wicked Witch's hat, $450; The Wizard's suit, $650; The Cowardly Lion's costume, $2,400; Dorothy's gingham dress, $1,000.

# A Town Called Hollywood

A TOWN CALLED HOLLYWOOD

## LANDMARKS PAST
## Once Upon a Time in a Hollywood Far, Far Away . . .

1. What restaurant was a favorite gathering place of the Hollywood press corps?

2. How did the Cocoanut Grove get its unusual decor?

3. There were four Brown Derby restaurants in the L.A. area. Which one was actually in the shape of a hat?
    a) Wilshire.   b) Vine Street.   c) Beverly Hills.   d) Los Feliz.

4. Located where the Comedy Store currently stands, this nightclub was one of Hollywood's most popular spots in the forties and fifties and was the site of several famous brawls.

5. In the 1930s the Colony Club, discreetly located on a side street off Sunset Boulevard, featured, along with major entertainers, unadvertised activity. What was it?

6. Gossip columnist Louella Parsons broadcast her famous 1930s radio program from a building that gave the show its name. What building was it?

7. On the current site of radio station KFAC once stood a favorite restaurant of James Dean. What was it called?

8. The North Rodeo Drive site of the original Romanoff's restaurant was turned into what private after-hours club in the mid-sixties?

9. Silent-film star Alla Nazimova's home, built in the early twenties, was converted in 1927 into a hotel that became a special favorite of the literary crowd in Hollywood. What was it called?

10. A one-time West Hollywood sheet-metal factory was, in 1967, turned into a short-lived but exclusive club that included bars, a dance floor, a pool room, and an art gallery. What was the club called?

ANSWERS

# LANDMARKS PAST
## Once Upon a Time in a Hollywood Far, Far Away...

1. The Cock 'n' Bull on the Sunset Strip. This English-pub-type restaurant, which opened in the early thirties, was probably popular with the press because it was frequented by cameramen, makeup artists, and other crew members, making it a good place to hear choice bits of insiders' studio gossip.

2. The maître d' of the Cocoanut Grove, which opened in the Ambassador Hotel in 1921, was an acquaintance of Rudolf Valentino. When he learned that there were several artificial palm trees left over from the filming of Valentino's *The Sheik* (1921), he acquired them cheaply and stocked the nightclub.

3. The original Brown Derby on Wilshire. The Vine Street Derby, however, was the place to be seen in the thirties and forties.

4. Ciro's, located on Sunset Boulevard. It was there that Errol Flynn was stabbed in the ear with a fork by the wife of Hollywood commentator Jimmy Fidler.

5. Gambling. The club's management was said to have ties with the infamous Detroit Purple Gang.

6. The Hollywood Hotel was the home of Parson's "Hollywood Hotel" program in the thirties. Today, that corner of Hollywood Boulevard and Highland Avenue houses a savings-and-loan high-rise.

7. The Villa Capri, located on Yucca Street in Hollywood until it closed in 1982.

8. The Daisy, a trendy spot that attracted the likes of Frank, Sammy, and the rest of their crowd.

9. The Garden of Allah, with its twenty-five guest cottages, was a haven for writers such as Dorothy Parker, Robert Benchley, F. Scott Fitzgerald, and George S. Kaufman, as well as for many actors and musicians.

10. The Factory. When celebrities didn't flock to it, the club was converted to the present Studio One, a Hollywood version of New York's Studio 54.

## MOVIES ABOUT HOLLYWOOD
## Looking in the Fun House Mirror

1. What 1976 comedy was inspired by the career of Rin Tin Tin?

2. In the 1976 film, *W. C. Fields and Me*, who did me refer to?

3. A prominent moment in the film *S.O.B.* (1981) involves a Hollywood director finally convincing his actress-wife to shed her angelic image and bare her breasts for a scene in his movie. What was ironic about this?

4. Perhaps the most popular movie musical of all time, this 1952 film was a spoof of Hollywood's difficult transition from silent to sound movies.

5. Former silent-film stars Buster Keaton, H. B. Warner, and Anna Q. Nilsson portray three former silent-film stars playing their weekly card game in what classic movie about Hollywood?

6. Both Marilyn Monroe and Ava Gardner were said to be the inspiration for this 1958 film about a Hollywood sex symbol.

7. Howard Hughes's chief attorney demanded a prerelease screening of this movie about a millionaire industrialist who takes over a Hollywood studio.

8. Frank Fane loses an Academy Award to Frank Sinatra in one of the trashiest movies ever made about Hollywood. What was it called?

9. This Hollywood superagent was said to be the model for Dyan Cannon's character in *The Last of Sheila* (1973).

10. The ruthless Hollywood producer in what 1952 movie was said to be loosely based on the life of David O. Selznick.

ANSWERS

# MOVIES ABOUT HOLLYWOOD
## Looking in the Fun House Mirror

1   *Won Ton Ton, the Dog Who Saved Hollywood.* It is uncertain whether or not Rinty's actual memoirs were used in the script.

2   Carlotta Monti, Fields's mistress for the last fourteen years of his life. Rod Steiger and Valerie Perrine played the title roles.

3   The "angel," actress Julie Andrews, was the real-life wife of *S.O.B.* director Blake Edwards.

4   *Singin' in the Rain.* Director-star Gene Kelly said, "Almost everything in *Singin' in the Rain* springs from the truth. It's a conglomeration of bits of movie lore."

5   *Sunset Boulevard* (1950).

6   *The Goddess.* Author Paddy Chayefsky denied it was about anyone in particular.

7   *The Carpetbaggers* (1964). Hughes's attorney decided to take no action because the story was so completely implausible.

8   *The Oscar* (1966). Sinatra, Merle Oberon, Edith Head, and Hedda Hopper were all persuaded to play themselves in the film.

9   Sue Mengers.

10  *The Bad and the Beautiful.* Selznick himself felt that while the character had mannerisms similar to his own, there was nothing in the film that related to his actual personal or professional life.

## THE PLACE IS FAMILIAR
## "Gosh Toto, I Don't Think We're in Kansas Any More."

1. Since its restoration in the 1970s, this grand old hotel—an early home of the Academy Awards presentations—has been used as a location for over two hundred films, TV movies, and commercials.

2. The complex known as Century City, on Los Angeles's Westside, was once a Twentieth Century-Fox back lot that was sold to developers in 1961. Why was it sold?

3. It was a primary setting in Arnold Schwarzenegger's first film, *Pumping Iron* (1977), and also the site of a Mr. America contest where Mae West gave out the prizes.

4. King Kong, Judy Garland, and Michael Jackson shared the stage (though not at the same time) of this huge downtown Los Angeles theater.

5. This Hollywood restaurant stands where Errol Flynn once slept.

6. In the film *Topper* (1937), many of the ghostly hijinks take place at the plush Seabreeze Hotel in Connecticut. The exterior used for the hotel was actually quite a different location. What and where was it?

7. The Mayfair Supermarket on Hyperion Avenue occupies the site of what was once one of the most "magical" places in Hollywood. What was it?

8. The movie *California Suite* (1978) is supposed to take place entirely at the famous Beverly Hills Hotel. How much of the hotel is actually used?

9. When D. W. Griffith's *The Birth of a Nation* (1915) opened at Clune's Auditorium in downtown Los Angeles, what bizarre gimmick was used to promote the movie?

10. The oldest church in Beverly Hills, it hosted Elizabeth Taylor's first wedding, Alfred Hitchcock's funeral, and the movie funeral of James Mason in the 1954 *A Star Is Born*.

ANSWERS

# THE PLACE IS FAMILIAR
## "Gosh Toto, I Don't Think We're in Kansas Any More."

1. The Biltmore Hotel on South Olive Street hosted the Oscars many times in the thirties and forties, and its own film credits include *Chinatown* (1974), *The Buddy Holly Story* (1978), *Splash* (1984), and remakes of *King Kong* (1976) and *A Star Is Born* (1976).

2. The studio was losing large amounts of money due to the ongoing production of *Cleopatra* (1963) and realized that the sale of the real estate would help pay a few bills.

3. Gold's Gym in Santa Monica.

4. The Shrine Auditorium, location of Kong's first appearance in captivity, Judy's closing speech in *A Star Is Born* (1954), and Michael's infamous fiery Pepsi commercial.

5. Butterfield's on Sunset Boulevard is located on property that was allegedly owned by John Barrymore; its dining room was once a guesthouse where Errol Flynn often stayed.

6. The rear entrance of Bullock's department store on Wilshire Boulevard in Los Angeles.

7. The original Walt Disney Studios occupied this spot until they moved to Burbank in 1940. Today, only a small marker in the parking lot commemorates the birthplace of Mickey Mouse and company.

8. It appears in one scene only—the terrace of Jane Fonda's room. All other hotel scenes were shot at the studio, because all public areas of the hotel (lobby, pool, the Polo Lounge) are off limits to film crews.

9. Outside the theater, actors dressed as Ku Klux Klansmen were assembled on horseback.

10. The Church of the Good Shepherd.

A TOWN CALLED HOLLYWOOD

# HISTORICAL HOLLYWOOD PLACES
## You Must Remember These . . .

1   In 1932 starlet Peg Entwistle leaped to her death from this structure, which was originally built to promote an unsuccessful real-estate venture.

2   Eighty years of makeup history, cosmetics ads, Hollywood photographs, and movie-star autographs can be viewed at this uniquely Hollywood place.

3   His studio, a two-story barn, became known as the place where Hollywood was born.

4   Hollywood's Hillcrest Country Club provided a regular lunchtime meeting place for a group of comedians that included Jack Benny, Groucho Marx, George Burns, Danny Kaye, and other greats. What did this group call itself?

5   What special attraction did Schwab's Drugstore hold for silent-film stars Charlie Chaplin and Harold Lloyd?

6   What Hollywood hotel was the favorite of black celebrities in the thirties?

7   This retirement home for ex-studio employees was opened in Woodland Hills in 1942 and added a hospital in 1948.

8   In 1982 Chateau Marmont Hotel was in the nation's headlines. Why?

9   In 1914 Carl Laemmle took over a large chicken ranch in the township of Lankershim, just over the Hollywood Hills, and relocated his new business there. What is this place known as today?

10  The set of Belshazzar's palace in D. W. Griffith's *Intolerance* (1916) and that of the castle in Douglas Fairbanks's *Robin Hood* (1922) hold what distinction?

ANSWERS

# HISTORICAL HOLLYWOOD PLACES
## You Must Remember These . . .

1  The HOLLYWOOD sign (which originally read HOLLYWOODLAND) on the side of Mount Lee.

2  The Max Factor Beauty Museum, in the Max Factor Building on North Highland Avenue.

3  Cecil B. DeMille rented the barn in 1913 and filmed *The Squaw Man*. It became one of the first nationwide box-office hits. The building was moved from its original location at Selma Avenue and Vine Street to 2300 Highland Avenue, where it still stands today.

4  The Hillcrest Round Table of Comedians. It was modeled after New York's Algonquin Round Table.

5  Chaplin and Lloyd, among the earliest of Schwab's regular patrons, spent a good deal of time in the pinball room in the back. Until the pinball machines were banned, many celebrities took part in spirited competitions, complete with cheering sections.

6  The Hotel Dunbar, which was declared a historical monument in 1974, was the place favored by blacks in entertainment and sports. It was the next door to the Club Alabam, which headlined the greatest black performers of the time, including Duke Ellington, Nat King Cole, and Dinah Washington.

7  The Motion Picture Country House.

8  Actor-comedian John Belushi was found dead of a drug overdose in one of its rooms.

9  Universal City, home of Universal Studios.

10  These are reputed to be the two largest sets ever created for a Hollywood film. Unsuccessful attempts were made to have the *Intolerance* set preserved as a monument.

A TOWN CALLED HOLLYWOOD

# SIGHTSEEING
## Okay, Everybody Back on the Bus!

1. Located on Hollywood Boulevard, this theater holds the distinction of being the first art deco–style movie theater.

2. Sid Grauman opened this theater in 1922, when the entire country was abuzz with the discovery of King Tut's tomb.

3. Many of Hollywood's most famous pets are buried here.

4. The Universal Studios Tour is one of Hollywood's (and the country's) most popular tourist attractions. When was it begun?

5. Formerly a nickelodeon, this is the oldest continually operating movie theater in Hollywood.

6. Due to a weird drawing of boundaries, this area, which became the location of many of Hollywood's hottest nightclubs in the thirties, is not part of Los Angeles and therefore not subject to the city's laws.

7. A private home two hundred miles from Hollywood was a favorite gathering place of celebrities in spite of its strictly enforced one-cocktail rule. Whose home was it?

8. A Hall of Presidents and a Chamber of Horrors are among the features of this Hollywood Boulevard attraction.

9. How did the tradition of putting stars' footprints in cement in front of Grauman's Chinese Theater begin?

10. What is "programmatic architecture"?

# SIGHTSEEING
## Okay, Everybody Back on the Bus!

1. The Pantages Theater opened in 1930. The theater hosted the Academy Awards ceremonies from 1949 to 1959.

2. The Egyptian Theater, which Grauman claimed was modeled after the temple in Thebes.

3. The SPCA Pet Memorial Park, in the San Fernando Valley, is the final resting place of Bogart's dog, Mae West's monkey, and Tonto's horses.

4. The modern tour began in 1963, but as early as 1915 the public, for 25 cents admission, was allowed to watch from the bleachers around certain outdoor sets.

5. The Hollywood Theater, said to have opened in 1911.

6. Sunset Strip, the mile-and-a-half stretch of Sunset Boulevard between West Hollywood and Beverly Hills.

7. William Randolph Hearst's San Simeon mansion. If a guest was caught smuggling in liquor, he would be informed by a secretary that he was leaving—unless he was a special friend of Hearst or companion Marion Davies.

8. Hollywood Wax Museum.

9. It was an accident. Douglas Fairbanks and Mary Pickford stepped on fresh cement in front of the theater and owner Sid Grauman asked them to sign their names.

10. The term refers to buildings whose forms reflect their names. The Brown Derby restaurant in the shape of a hat is the most famous example of this style in Los Angeles.

A TOWN CALLED HOLLYWOOD

# A GOOD PLACE TO BE SEEN
## A Quiet Little Table for Twenty

1. The Cafe Gala, opened on Sunset Boulevard in 1941, was known for its:
   a) Outrageous cover charge.   b) After-hours celebrity parties.
   c) Predominantly gay bar.   d) Salad bar.

2. This well-known hangout in a famous Hollywood hotel was once a children's nursery.

3. Tom Mix often dined by a window of this Hollywood Boulevard eatery, a favorite of silent-film stars, so his fans would be sure to see him.

4. Hollywood's most popular ballroom in the twenties and thirties, it was known for its Charleston contests and Saturday afternoon tea dances.

5. In the 1930s and 1940s, Friday nights at the Vine Street Brown Derby were unique: the restaurant would be packed early, empty out at eight o'clock, and then fill up again later. What caused the mid-evening exodus?

6. What Rodeo Drive restaurant made it easiest for patrons to see and be seen?

7. From the thirties through the fifties, this screenwriter's Santa Monica home was a meeting place for the European artists and intellectuals of Hollywood.

8. Why did Hollywood and Vine become the most famous intersection in the world?

9. When this still-popular Hollywood restaurant opened it 1936, it was known as the Southern Pit. What is it now called?

10. He was discovered at a tea dance at the Hollywood Roosevelt Hotel in the twenties.

ANSWERS

# A GOOD PLACE TO BE SEEN
## A Quiet Little Table for Twenty

1  After-hours celebrity parties and predominantly gay bar.

2  The Polo Lounge in the Beverly Hills Hotel. The hotel was temporarily closed in the early years of the Depression and the nursery was converted for the reopening in 1933.

3  Musso and Frank Grill, located at 6667 Hollywood Boulevard since 1919.

4  The Montmartre Cafe on Hollywood Boulevard. Joan Crawford was often an enthusiastic participant in the Charleston contests.

5  The Derby was just a short walk from the American Legion Stadium, where the Friday night fights were held. The Hollywood crowd would gather at the restaurant, go over to watch the boxing, and return after the feature fight was over.

6  Romanoff's, which was started on investments from its Hollywood clientele, had its hexagonal main room arranged without any private corners and gave every booth a clear view of the room's entrance. This allowed everyone in the place to know what everyone else was doing—and with whom.

7  Salka Viertel, co-author of two Greta Garbo classics, *Queen Christina* (1933) and *Conquest* (1937), often entertained Igor Stravinsky, Thomas Mann, Charlie Chaplin, Sergei Eisenstein, and others.

8  In the 1930s, there were many radio stations located on Vine Street, and programs originating there commonly opened with ". . . brought to you from Hollywood and Vine." To listeners in homes all over America, these words came to symbolize all that was magical about Hollywood.

9  Chasen's. It was originally a shack on Beverly Boulevard, with a barbecue pit dug in the backyard. Owner Dave Chasen later expanded the building to the point of installing a second-floor steam bath for his many famous patrons.

10 Lew Ayres, who promptly signed a six-month contract with Pathé.

# HOLLYWOOD PAYS THE MORTGAGE
## Not-So-Humble Abodes

1. On his ranch in Jupiter, Florida, this Hollywood actor had a treehouse built complete with Japanese bath and full kitchen.

2. Charlie Chaplin's Hollywood home became known as the "Breakaway House." Why?

3. To the disappointment of many of his houseguests, this Hollywood director's bathroom did not sport solid-gold fixtures or hot and cold running rose water.

4. In 1982 this actor bought Charlie Chaplin's Breakaway House.

5. In the left column is the original owner of a Hollywood home. Match it with the later resident of the home in the right column.
   - Natalie and Buster Keaton.      Donald O'Connor.
   - John Gilbert.                    Peter and Pat Lawford.
   - Joan Crawford.                   James and Pamela Mason.
   - Louis B. Mayer's beach house.    Elton John.

6. In Jayne Mansfield's home in the fifties, what did the sex star's heart-shaped swimming pool, toilet seat, and wall-to-wall carpeting have in common?

7. Name the silent-film cowboy who had his initials in neon lights on the roof of his Beverly Hills home.

8. Name the Academy Award–winning actor-producer-director who lives at the Beverly Wilshire Hotel.

9. His home, Falcon Lair, above Benedict Canyon, featured his collection of medieval armor and antique weapons.

10. After they were married in 1939, Hollywood's number one couple bought a ranch in Encino. Who were they?

ANSWERS

# HOLLYWOOD PAYS THE MORTGAGE
## Not-So-Humble Abodes

1. Burt Reynolds. The exterior of the house is painted in camouflage colors, to blend in with the surroundings.

2. Chaplin, noted for his frugality, had studio carpenters help with the construction of his estate. The set builders were used to putting up temporary structures, so before long his house was coming apart.

3. Cecil B. DeMille. The director was noted for lavish bathroom scenes in his movies. His own home was modest by his own movie standards.

4. George Hamilton.

5. Natalie and Buster Keaton.    James and Pamela Mason.
   John Gilbert.                 Elton John.
   Joan Crawford.                Donald O'Connor.
   Louis B. Mayer's beach house. Peter and Pat Lawford.

6. They were all pink. Everything, from her car to the ceiling in her living room, was in the actress's favorite color.

7. Tom Mix. In an incredible display of vulgarity, the actor plastered his monogram over fireplaces, on the gates to his driveway, and on his front door.

8. Warren Beatty prefers a no-strings-attached life style and opts for a penthouse at the swank hotel over a mansion in Bel Air.

9. Rudolph Valentino. His estate was named for the screenplay, *The Hooded Falcon*, written by his wife, Natacha Rambova.

10. Clark Gable and Carole Lombard preferred to live away from glittery Beverly Hills or Bel Air. Their home was furnished in Early American to suit Gable's taste.

A TOWN CALLED HOLLYWOOD

# HOLLYWOOD GOES SHOPPING
## As Time Goes . . . Buy!

1. This confectioner, located just a block away from Grauman's Chinese Theater, has been a favorite of the stars since 1929.

2. The May Company department store in Los Angeles was sued by actress Hedy Lamarr for $5 million in 1966. Why?

3. Douglas Fairbanks bought this former hunting lodge as a wedding present for his bride in 1920. What was it called?

4. The most expensive diamond ever owned by Liz Taylor was how many carats?
    a) 29.70.   b) 33.19.   c) 45.15.   d) 69.42.

5. Frederick's of Hollywood, internationally known for its collection of sexy underwear, has a line of musical panties. Which of the following songs is the largest seller?
    a) "Strangers in the Night."   b) "Here Comes the Bride."
    c) "Happy Birthday."   d) "The Stripper."

6. After making Mae West's costumes for *Every Day's a Holiday* (1937), this Italian designer marketed a perfume in a bottle shaped like the hourglass figure of the star. The scent was called Shocking. Name the designer of the dresses and perfume.

7. Clark Gable unintentionally caused a depression in the sales of this garment in the 1930s.

8. Bette Davis shopped for her personal wardrobe at this fashionable store.

9. Name the film in which Joan Crawford wore a tulle gown that started a stampede to local department stores, with thousands of women buying copies of the dress.

10. Name the Hollywood superstar who drove a Volkswagen beetle instead of the usual Mercedes or Rolls.

ANSWERS

# HOLLYWOOD GOES SHOPPING
## As Time Goes . . . Buy!

1   C. C. Brown's, located at 7007 Hollywood Boulevard.

2   She had been arrested in the store for allegedly shoplifting $86 worth of merchandise. After she was acquitted, she sued for damages, but the suit was dismissed.

3   Known as Pickfair, the twenty-two-room mansion was home to Fairbanks and wife Mary Pickford until their divorce in 1935. She got to keep it.

4   The 69.42-carat Cartier-Burton diamond cost Richard Burton over $1,050,000.

5   "Happy Birthday."

6   Schiaparelli. When the dresses for Miss West arrived from the designer's Paris salon they proved to be inches too small for the buxom West. Costume fitters at Paramount worked feverishly to refit the designer originals.

7   Men's undershirts. When sexy Clark Gable was filmed not wearing an undershirt in *It Happened One Night* (1934), wives all over America stopped buying their spouses the undergarment.

8   I. Magnin.

9   *Letty Lynton* (1932). The Adrian creation, which sported huge tulle sleeves, was designed to hide the flaws in Crawford's figure: broad shoulders, wide hips, and short legs.

10  Paul Newman. The car did have a Porsche engine, however.

# HOLLYWOOD GETS RELIGION
## God Is My Co-Star

1. This film villain's varied life included success in silent films, impoverishment with the advent of sound, an eventual return to Hollywood fame in a 1957 role, and ordination as a Zen priest in his later years.

2. *Inchon* (1982), a movie that tells the story of Gen. Douglas MacArthur's exploits in the Korean War, was financed by a distinctly non-Hollywood person, who also served as the film's technical advisor. Who?

3. What actor-turned-writer worked for Walt Disney, and later starred in a contemporary religious epic before becoming a best-selling novelist in the seventies?

4. An indoor set reputed to be the world's largest was built for *The Agony and the Ecstasy* (1965). What did the set depict?

5. Screenwriter Paul Schrader, whose script credits include *Taxi Driver* (1976) and *Raging Bull* (1980), did not see his first movie until he was seventeen years old. Why?

6. When Horace and Daeida Wilcox founded Hollywood in 1887, they never envisioned that it would one day become Tinsel Town. What plans did they have for the new settlement?

7. In 1953 this actress opted not to renew her contract with Twentieth Century-Fox and instead entered a convent.

8. Loretta Young gave this reason for not marrying Spencer Tracy.

9. Name the 1923 film that Cecil B. DeMille produced as a result of a national contest that asked the public to send in plot ideas for movies they would most like to see.

10. Catholic bishops across the country formed this censoring committee in 1933.

ANSWERS

# HOLLYWOOD GETS RELIGION
## God Is My Co-Star

1. Sessue Hayakawa, whose portrayal of the evil Colonel Saito in *The Bridge on the River Kwai* (1957) was the pinnacle of his many-faceted career.

2. The Reverend Sun Myung Moon, leader of the Unification Church.

3. Tom Tryon. He starred on television in Disney's "Tales of the Texas Rangers," played the title role in *The Cardinal* (1963), and wrote *The Other* and *Crowned Heads*, among other scary novels.

4. It re-created the interior of the Sistine Chapel for this spectacle about the artist Michelangelo.

5. He grew up in a very strict Calvinist family and was not permitted to indulge in such activities.

6. They hoped Hollywood would become a religious community. Prohibitionists, they banned liquor from the town and offered free land to anyone willing to build a church.

7. June Haver became a novitiate of the Sisters of Charity for seven months. In 1955 she married Fred MacMurray.

8. Ms. Young said she would not break up Tracy's marriage because they were both devout Catholics and would face excommunication from the church.

9. *The Ten Commandments*. Many of the responses to DeMille's contest called for a religious movie. Eight of the thousands of entries specified they wanted DeMille to produce a picture about Moses and the Ten Commandments.

10. The National Legion of Decency. The legion reviewed all new films and classified them as "Passed," "Objectionable in Part," or "Condemned." Catholics attending movies on the Condemned list were committing a venial sin.

# HOLLYWOOD GOES TO SCHOOL
## Reading, Writing, and Rehearsals

1. What do Joel McCrea, Sally Kellerman, *Los Angeles Times* publisher Norman Chandler, and Nobel Prize–winning scientist William Schockley all have in common?

2. Started in 1930 as the Hollywood Conservatory of Music and Arts, this school went on to change its name and turn out students that included Natalie Wood, Ryan O'Neal, and a number of Mouseketeers.

3. Three statues in front of Venice High School depict the "physical," the "mental," and the "spiritual." All were modeled for by students, one of whom went on to much greater fame in Hollywood. Who?

4. His hometown paper, the *Modesto Bee*, ran a front-page photo of the 1962 car crash that almost ended this future director's life before his film career could begin.

5. The art deco facade of Venice High School appears in the opening scenes of what popular teenage movie?

6. In the twenties, the Lawlor School operated out of the second floor of a building on Hollywood Boulevard. What was unique about this school?

7. At nine years of age, he was sent off to Dunstable school in Bedfordshire, England.

8. When he told his father he wanted to be an actor, his father had him transferred out of Hollywood High and into a business college.

9. At Glendale Union High School in the twenties he played on the football team, was head of the Latin Society, sat on the debating team, and managed to be an *A* student. Who was he?

10. Name the actress who attended St. Agnes School in Kansas City in 1917 as a child.

ANSWERS

# HOLLYWOOD GOES TO SCHOOL
## Reading, Writing, and Rehearsals

1. All were once students at Hollywood High School. Others who attended include Lana Turner, Jason Robards, James Garner, and John Ritter, to name a few.

2. The Hollywood Professional School, on Hollywood Boulevard, still has classes until 12:45 only—to allow time for performers to work in the afternoon.

3. Venice High School student Myrna Williams, who later changed her name to Myrna Loy, modeled for the "spiritual" statue.

4. George Lucas, then a high-school senior, miraculously survived the crash that wrapped his Fiat around a walnut tree. He re-created life in Modesto eleven years later in *American Graffiti* (1973).

5. *Grease* (1978).

6. It was a school for child performers attended by Judy Garland and Mickey Rooney, among others. The building it occupied later became the Hollywood Professional School.

7. Gary Cooper, whose father had been a barrister in England.

8. Lon Chaney, Jr. The senior Chaney disapproved of his son's acting ambitions and wanted him to be a respected businessman.

9. Marion Morrison, later known as John Wayne.

10. Joan Crawford was sent to a convent school when her mother divorced her second husband.

## HOLLYWOOD STYLE
## Nothing Succeeds Like Excess

1. The press book for this 1964 film proclaimed: "Sidney Poitier in his first non-Negro role!"

2. This picture's credits included the immortal line, "Script by William Shakespeare, Additional Dialogue by Samuel Taylor."

3. Where did Clark Gable propose to Carole Lombard?

4. Her marriage to a doctor gave this columnist an inside line to lab test results that allowed her to be the first to announce pregnancies of the stars.

5. When Marion Davies left MGM to work for Warner Brothers, she was adamant that she could not be housed in any structure other than her bungalow on the MGM lot. How was this resolved?

6. In 1940, *Hollywood Reporter* owner Billy Wilkerson was challenged to a duel by F. Scott Fitzgerald. Why?

7. While living in her luxurious apartment in the Ravenswood building on North Rossmore Avenue, Mae West decided that she didn't like the color of the building across the street, which her apartment looked out on. What did she do about it?

8. Even Walt Disney proved not to be exempt from censorship when his 1954 Academy Award–winning documentary, *The Vanishing Prairie*, was called "indecent" and banned by New York censors. What did they object to?

9. Name the Pathé Pictures studio head who insisted that Carole Lombard, at 121 pounds, was too fat.

10. A divorce is essential to belong to this all-female Hollywood organization.

ANSWERS

# HOLLYWOOD STYLE
## Nothing Succeeds Like Excess

1  *The Long Ships*. Poitier played a Moorish chief who battled the Vikings.

2  *The Taming of the Shrew* (1929), which starred Mary Pickford and Douglas Fairbanks.

3  In booth 54 of the Vine Street Brown Derby.

4  Louella Parsons, wife of Dr. Harry "Docky" Martin.

5  Davies's paramour, William Randolph Hearst, had the bungalow cut into three parts and towed from the MGM lot in Culver City to Warner's Burbank studio.

6  The *Reporter* had published an editorial demanding that Fitzgerald's lover, columnist Sheilah Graham, be kicked out of Hollywood.

7  Legend has it that she bought the building and had it repainted..

8  A scene that showed a buffalo giving birth. The stunned Disney commented: "It would be a shame if New York children had to believe the stork brings buffaloes, too." The censors later reversed themselves.

9  Joseph P. Kennedy. Kennedy told Ms. Lombard to shed the extra poundage. Carole lost ten pounds, but not before telling Kennedy, "You're not so skinny yourself."

10  LADIES (Life After Divorce Is Eventually Sane), a self-help group created by Hollywood ex-wives. Some of the ex-wives are Marion Segal, former mate of George Segal, Jackie Joseph, the ex of Ken Berry, and Patti Lewis, one-time spouse of Jerry Lewis.

## THE STAR TREATMENT
## "Room Service? Send up a Room!"

1. Who designed the wedding gown Liz Taylor wore for her first marriage (to Nicky Hilton)?

2. At which Hollywood cemetery did the Lady in Black leave flowers on Rudolph Valentino's grave each year?

3. When the subject of this 1941 film biography attended its opening in New York, he was greeted with a ticker-tape parade, a trainload of senators from Washington, and a half-minute blackout of the lights on Broadway.

4. When Howard Hughes wanted to meet RKO contract star Jean Simmons and she refused to see him, how did he go about getting his way?

5. In 1919 this movie queen bought a lavish home across from the Beverly Hills Hotel.

6. When Ginger Rogers was appearing in the 1930 Broadway play *Girl Crazy* with Fred Astaire, what unique plan did she devise for arriving at the theater on time?

7. Claudette Colbert was so particular about one aspect of her film work that she would demand entire sets be rebuilt to accommodate her. What was her fetish?

8. Louis B. Mayer gave Elizabeth Taylor this gift after she starred in the movie *National Velvet* (1944).

9. Name the actor who is one of the few in his profession to be allowed to join the blue-blooded Los Angeles Country Club.

10. What do these stars have in common: Olive Borden, Ronald Colman, Louise Fazenda, Preston Foster, Burt Lancaster, Edward Sedgwick, Ernest Torrence, and Joanne Woodward?

ANSWERS

# THE STAR TREATMENT
## "Room Service? Send up a Room!"

1. The famous Edith Head did the gown, which was a "gift" from MGM. The studio was happy to promote the wedding in connection with her concurrent on-screen wedding in *Father of the Bride* (1950).

2. Hollywood Memorial Park. Valentino has plenty of Hollywood biggies resting in peace with him at Memorial Park: Marion Davies, Cecil B. DeMille, Nelson Eddy, and Douglas Fairbanks, to name a few.

3. *Sergeant York.*

4. Hughes bought RKO, making Simmons his employee.

5. Gloria Swanson, who believed in flaunting her wealth. She lived like a queen and was reputed to have spent upward of $100,000 on her wardrobe in a single year.

6. Rogers beat the New York traffic by hiring an ambulance to rush her to the theater.

7. Ms. Colbert insisted on being photographed only from the left, which she considered to be her best side.

8. The studio head gave the youthful Taylor the horse who "co-starred" with her in the film. When the star was older, studio heads and directors were expected to give the actress diamonds in appreciation of her appearing in their films.

9. Randolph Scott, whose ancestors were early Virginia settlers.

10. They were the first eight stars to have their names immortalized on Hollywood Boulevard's Walk of Fame in 1958.

# BACKBITING
## Some Prime Cuts

1. When Samuel Goldwyn saw Bette Davis's first screen test in 1929 for the movie *Raffles*, his reaction was:
    a) That dame smokes too much.
    b) Great eyes but she's got a lousy figure.   c) Who did this to me?
    d) Bring me Barabbas.

2. When Brando had an appendicitis attack while filming *A Countess from Hong Kong* (1967), the cast sent him a bouquet. Whose signature was missing from the get well card?

3. When Tallulah Bankhead said that this star was "as pure as the driven slush," who was she talking about?

4. Why did columnist Hedda Hopper and the American Legion denounce Kirk Douglas's production of *Spartacus* (1960)?

5. Groucho Marx gave this explanation for avoiding a certain movie star's films: "I never see movies where the man's tits are bigger than the woman's." Who was the well-endowed actor?

6. When Katharine Hepburn's longtime boyfriend Leland Hayward married Margaret Sullavan, Kate sent a congratulatory telegram to Sullavan. How did Sullavan respond?

7. Samuel Goldwyn is quoted as saying, "So many people came to his funeral because they wanted to make sure the S.O.B. was dead." Who was he talking about?

8. According to his son Gary, this actor punished his four sons with a metal-studded belt.

9. When it was announced that Olivia de Havilland would replace this star of *Hush, Hush, Sweet Charlotte* (1965), Bette Davis celebrated by posing with a bottle of Coke. Who was the star de Havilland replaced?

10. When Ginger Rogers replaced the ailing Judy Garland in *The Barkleys of Broadway* (1949), what "gift" did Garland give Ginger to wish her good luck?

ANSWERS

# BACKBITING
## Some Prime Cuts

1. Who did this to me? Mr. Goldwyn was not impressed with Ms. Davis.

2. Co-star Sophia Loren, who was less than enamored with her acting partner.

3. Herself.

4. Douglas hired a victim of the McCarthy-era blacklist, Dalton Trumbo, to do the screenplay and allowed the writer's name to appear in the credits.

5. Victor Mature.

6. She ripped up the wire and threw it away.

7. Louis B. Mayer.

8. Bing Crosby's role as a disciplinarian is described in detail in son Gary's biography, *Going My Own Way*.

9. Joan Crawford, who had Pepsi Cola machines installed on her movie sets, after she married Alfred Stills, chairman of the board of Pepsi.

10. Garland sent Rogers, whose face was covered with peach fuzz, a gold-edged shaving mug.

# DEATH IN HOLLYWOOD
## Final Fade-Outs

1. This former studio chief was buried in a Hollywood Memorial Cemetery plot that was specially selected to allow him to keep an eye on his studio.

2. Elizabeth Short, victim of a grisly murder in 1947, was known around Hollywood by a name that referred to the color she always wore. What was she called?

3. If Elizabeth Taylor had accompanied her husband Mike Todd on a 1958 trip from Los Angeles to New York, she would have died in the plane crash that killed him. What prevented her from taking the ill-fated flight?

4. Who is Thomas T. Noguchi?

5. How did London's theater district pay tribute to Vivien Leigh on the night of her death in July of 1967?

6. Slumberland, Babyland, and Inspiration Slope are all areas of what popular tourist attraction?

7. This sexy film star of the silents claimed her name was an anagram for Arab Death.

8. When Jean Harlow married MGM executive Paul Bern, their short-lived violent marriage ended in Bern's suicide. What was rumored to be the reason for his taking his own life?

9. Following his death, relatives of this famous movie director retained his personal staff and kept his estate intact.

10. Actor Wallace Reid was put in a sanitarium due to his addiction to morphine. He died in a padded cell almost a year later in 1923. What did his actress-wife Dorothy Reid do as a lasting memory for her husband?

ANSWERS

# DEATH IN HOLLYWOOD
## Final Fade-Outs

1. Harry Cohn. Unfortunately for Cohn, in 1972 Columbia moved their North Gower Street studios to Burbank.

2. The Black Dahlia. Her murder—she was found sliced in half at the waist—was never solved. In 1975 it was the subject of a TV movie, *Who Is the Black Dahlia?*

3. She was bedridden with a fever and a bad case of bronchitis, so her doctor would not allow her to go.

4. The former chief medical examiner of Los Angeles County, known as the Coroner of the Stars, who investigated the deaths of Marilyn Monroe, Natalie Wood, and William Holden, among others.

5. All the West End theaters darkened their exterior lights for one hour that night.

6. Forest Lawn Cemetery in Glendale, where countless Hollywood stars, as well as baseball's Casey Stengel, are buried.

7. Theda Bara, known as The Vamp. Her early publicity pictures often showed her with a human skull, no doubt one of her amorous victims.

8. It is believed Bern was sexually impotent and was bitter when sex goddess Harlow was unable to help him.

9. Cecil B. DeMille. Each day, DeMille's elderly secretary came to the estate to work on family business. She turned the calendar to the current date and put fresh flowers on the desk of her late boss.

10. Widow Reid starred in an exposé of the drug world, *Human Wreckage* (1923). To make the most of her situation, she was billed as Mrs. Wallace Reid.

# HOBBIES
## Polo, Anyone?

1. Who is Forrest J. Ackerman?

2. On any given weekend in the 1930s, such Hollywood luminaries as Spencer Tracy, Leslie Howard, Jack Warner, and Walt Disney would gather at Will Rogers's Pacific Palisades estate (now a state park) to enjoy what athletic pastime?

3. This refined lawn game was popular in Beverly Hills in the 1930s, especially at the homes of movie moguls like Darryl F. Zanuck and Samuel Goldwyn.

4. This horror-film star, together with his wife Mary, has authored several cookbooks.

5. Name the actor whose estate, the Belle Vista, was home to a host of animals: opossums, a monkey, Siamese cats, and several greyhounds and St. Bernards, to name a few of the residents.

6. Before she adopted the first of her four children, actress Joan Crawford collected over two thousand of these.

7. Name the actress who in her late teens won a bronze medal for figure skating at the Madison Square Garden Skating Club.

8. Paul Newman did not have a double for the movie *Winning* (1969). What sport did he master in order to do his own stunts?

9. When actor Randolph Scott got the lead in the western *Wild Horse Mesa* (1932), he had no experience as a cowboy but he did look good on a horse. Where had he learned how to ride?

10. Ruby Keeler, tap-dancing star of *42nd Street* (1933), has won trophies for her prowess at this sport.

ANSWERS

# HOBBIES
## Polo, Anyone?

1. Reputedly the world's greatest collector of science-fiction and horror-film memorabilia. His basement in L.A. is said to contain 125,000 movie stills, as well as such rare artifacts as the cape from the original *Dracula* (1931) and a part of King Kong's paw.

2. They played polo on Rogers's regulation-sized field.

3. Croquet.

4. Vincent Price and Mary Grant Price share a common interest in gourmet cooking and have written, among others, *A Treasury of Great Recipes* and *A National Treasury of Cooking*.

5. The animal-loving John Barrymore. The estate also sported an aviary filled with three hundred birds.

6. Dolls. Prior to becoming a real mother Crawford gave the dolls to various L.A. hospitals.

7. The ever-athletic Katharine Hepburn.

8. Race-car driving. Newman enrolled at the Bob Bondurant school to learn to race competitively. After making the movie, racing became a passion with Newman.

9. The aristocratic actor had ridden in fox hunts as a child growing up in Virginia.

10. Golf.

A TOWN CALLED HOLLYWOOD

# ODD JOBS OF THE RICH AND FAMOUS
## We Knew Them When

1. One of the jobs Dustin Hoffman had before becoming an actor was:
   a) Psychiatric attendant.   b) French frier at McDonald's.
   c) Stock boy at Macy's.   d) Brilliant young attorney.

2. If there hadn't been a slump in the world tea market, this character actor might not have given up his career as a tea planter in Ceylon (now Sri Lanka), and he and Bogie would never have met in Casablanca.

3. Match the actor with the job he had before reaching stardom.
   Wallace Beery.            Gold miner.
   George Segal.             Real-estate salesman.
   Victor McLaglen.          Trapeze artist.
   Walter Brennan.           Jazz musician.
   Yul Brynner.              Elephant trainer.

4. Long before he played opposite Bette Davis and Rita Hayworth, he was cleaning out stables for Will Rogers.

5. Studio head Harry Cohn promoted this actress as the Lavendar Lady. While living in Chicago she had a less glamourous existence as a model demonstrating refrigerators.

6. Born in Pennsylvania, this movie tough guy was a coal miner at the age of sixteen:
   a) Sylvester Stallone.   b) Charles Bronson.   c) Clint Eastwood.
   d) George Raft.

7. Before winning an Oscar for her performance in *Alice Doesn't Live Here Anymore* (1975), she was a Gleason Girl on television's "The Jackie Gleason Show."

8. If you went for a swim at Rockaway Beach in New York in the early fifties, chances are this future star was looking out for your safety.

9. It comes as no surprise that Gene Kelly was a dance instructor, but what other job did he have as well:
   a) Magazine editor.   b) Apprentice bricklayer.   c) Tree trimmer.
   d) Chimney sweep.

10. Although we tend to think of him in his movie role wearing leather boots and standing in front of an American flag, this actor once had the unlikely job of teaching in an all-woman's college in Columbus, Missouri.

ANSWERS

# ODD JOBS OF THE RICH AND FAMOUS
## We Knew Them When

1  Psychiatric attendant.

2  Sydney Greenstreet.

3  Wallace Beery, elephant trainer; George Segal, jazz musician; Victor McLaglen, gold miner; Walter Brennan, real-estate salesman; Yul Brynner, trapeze artist.

4  Glenn Ford.

5  Kim Novak.

6  Charles Bronson.

7  Ellen Burstyn.

8  James Caan was a lifeguard during his high school days in New York.

9  Apprentice bricklayer.

10  General Patton himself, George C. Scott.

# There's No Business Like

THERE'S NO BUSINESS LIKE

# SCREENWRITERS
## Read It and Weep

1. Although better known as a brilliant comedian and comic actor, he received a screenwriting credit on the Mel Brooks comedy western *Blazing Saddles* (1974).

2. One of Hollywood's most successful screenwriters, I. A. L. Diamond's credits include *Some Like It Hot* (1959), *The Apartment* (1960), *Irma la Douce* (1963), and *The Fortune Cookie* (1966), among many others. But what does I. A. L. stand for?

3. The most in-demand screenwriter of the 1970s made his debut as a writer-director on *Personal Best* (1982). Who is he?

4. Neil Simon, well respected as both a screenwriter and a playwright, was also a top television writer of the 1950s. Which of the following shows did he *not* write for:
    a) "Your Show of Shows" (Sid Caesar).
    b) "Caesar's Hour."
    c) "You'll Never Get Rich" (a.k.a. "Sgt. Bilko").
    d) "The Honeymooners" (Jackie Gleason).
    e) "The Garry Moore Show."

5. Screenwriter Paddy Chayefsky wrote the first television script to be made into a motion picture. What was it called?

6. Between 1954 and 1956, screenwriter John Michael Hayes worked on four consecutive films for one very famous director, but then had a falling out with him and the two never spoke to each other again. Who was the director?

7. This screenwriter, who has written several of the most wildly popular films of the 1980s, was a Chicago advertising copywriter before Steven Spielberg read one of his scripts.

8. A competent actor as well as a highly successful screenwriter, he has appeared in several of the films he has written and was perhaps most memorable as a hotel desk clerk in *The Graduate* (1967).

9. Writer Herman Mankiewicz had a famous dispute with Orson Welles over who should get the screen credit for writing *Citizen Kane* (1941), a credit they eventually shared. At one point, however, Mankiewicz decided he did not want to be known as the writer. Why?

10. Screenwriter Hal Kanter's debut as a director on a 1957 film he also wrote was overshadowed by the fact that it starred a leading man who was to get *all* the publicity on *every* film he did. Who?

ANSWERS

# SCREENWRITERS
## Read It and Weep

1   Richard Pryor.

2   International Algebra League. Itek (his real first name) was a math prodigy as a child.

3   Robert Towne, whose credits include *The Last Detail* (1973), *Chinatown* (1974), and *Shampoo* (1975).

4   Simon did not write for "The Honeymooners."

5   *Marty* (1955). Originally written as a 1953 "NBC Playhouse" production, it was made into the 1955 movie starring Ernest Borgnine. Chayefsky expressed his later feelings about television in his screenplay for *Network* (1976).

6   Alfred Hitchcock. He wanted Hayes to share the screenplay credit on *The Man Who Knew Too Much* (1956) with the film's technical advisor, but Hayes refused. He had also written *Rear Window* (1954), *To Catch a Thief* (1955), and *The Trouble with Harry* (1955).

7   Lawrence Kasdan, whose credits include *Raiders of the Lost Ark* (1981), *The Empire Strikes Back* (1980), and *Return of the Jedi* (1983), first impressed Spielberg with his script for the comedy *Continental Divide* (1981).

8   Buck Henry, whose writing credits also include *Catch-22* (1970) and, more recently, *Protocol* (1984).

9   He was afraid of retribution from William Randolph Hearst, on whom everyone felt the movie was based.

10   Elvis Presley in *Loving You*. Kanter's credits include *The Road To Bali* (1952), *Pocketful of Miracles* (1961), and *Move Over, Darling* (1963).

## DISCOVERIES
## Where Have You Been All My Life?

1. While a University of Texas freshman in 1968, she won a beauty contest and her picture was sent to Hollywood, attracting the attention of a publicist there. Who was she?

2. Which beautiful leading lady was first discovered while playing baseball as a twelve-year-old tomboy?

3. Name the major star who was discovered while working on horseback as a cowboy extra in the 1920s?

4. What ex-chorus girl was discovered on a night in 1954 when she replaced the ailing star in the Broadway show *The Pajama Game*?

5. A sixteen-year-old chorus girl was first noticed when she played a "beaded bag" in a "Living Curtain" stage number and "Labor Day" in a holiday routine. Who was she?

6. What handsome leading man was a truck driver for the Budget Pack Company when another driver arranged a meeting for him with a Hollywood agent?

7. This TV-star-turned-movie-star was discovered in 1962 by fellow-actor Richard Egan. Who was he?

8. What female silent-movie star got her start by winning a contest that offered a film role as a prize?

9. He was featured in an obscure New York play, *The Wind Is Ninety*, when his friend Lauren Bacall urged producer Hal Wallis to consider him for a leading role.

10. What leading man was first noticed on the Fox lot in 1928, while loading furniture from a warehouse onto a truck?

ANSWERS

# DISCOVERIES
## Where Have You Been All My Life?

1  Farrah Fawcett. Publicist David Mirisch had to convince Farrah's parents to allow her to come to Hollywood.

2  Carole Lombard. Director Alan Dwan saw her playing outside the Los Angeles home of a friend in 1921.

3  Gary Cooper, a bit player in numerous western shorts, was signed as an extra for *The Winning of Barbara Worth* (1926), but ended up making a strong impression when he filled in for one of the main supporting actors.

4  Shirley MacLaine. Alfred Hitchcock's associate, Herbert Coleman, was in the audience and went backstage to meet her. He arranged a screen test the next day, and Shirley won a leading role in *The Trouble with Harry* (1955). Hal Wallis had seen her earlier and arranged a screen test that led to a contract, but this was her first movie.

5  Joan Crawford. Producer Harry Rapf picked her out of a chorus of forty-five dancers appearing in a New York show called *Innocent Eyes* in 1924.

6  Agent Harry Willson changed the driver's name to Rock Hudson and started him off on his career.

7  Ryan O'Neal. He met Egan at the gym where they both worked out.

8  Clara Bow won first prize in the Fame and Fortune Contest sponsored by Brewster Publications in Brooklyn in 1921.

9  Kirk Douglas. Wallis then co-starred him with Barbara Stanwyck in *The Strange Love of Martha Ivers* (1946).

10  John Wayne, then a studio propman, was spotted by director Raoul Walsh.

THERE'S NO BUSINESS LIKE

# THE STUDIOS AND THEIR CHIEFS
## The Head Honchos

1  Why did MGM's Irving Thalberg threaten Greta Garbo with the remark: "If she turns down this role I will stop her paycheck"?

2  Name the studio that was formed by a group of silent-screen stars?

3  What studio head was put on Hitler's extinction list?

4  This studio chief was known for his "clout" in more ways than one.

5  What studio head began his career writing scripts for Rin Tin Tin?

6  Why did Sam Goldwyn never carry money in his pockets?

7  David O. Selznick brought what famous Englishman to work in America for the first time?

8  Which studio head was the hardest to meet with?

9  In a business that abounded with coldhearted men, the head of Columbia was generally acclaimed as the meanest and most feared in Hollywood. Who was he?

10 Born in Warsaw, Poland, this studio chief later lived in England and served as a blacksmith's assistant before coming to America at age fifteen to seek his fortune. Who was he?

ANSWERS

# THE STUDIOS AND THEIR CHIEFS
## The Head Honchos

1. Garbo had refused to take the title role in *Anna Christie* (1930) because she felt the film denigrated Swedes. She eventually accepted the part and was a hit in her first talkie.

2. United Artists was formed in 1919 by Douglas Fairbanks, Mary Pickford, Charlie Chaplin, and D. W. Griffith, prompting Metro executive Richard Rowland's famous remark, "The lunatics have taken charge of the asylum."

3. Jack Warner, because of his film *Confessions of a Nazi Spy* (1939). Warner also claimed that mobster Bugsy Siegel had come to him offering to do away with Nazi officers Goebbels and Goering.

4. Louis B. Mayer, never one to back down from a conflict, on various occasions punched out the likes of Charlie Chaplin, Erich von Stroheim, and Sam Goldwyn, the latter in the showers of the Hillcrest Country Club.

5. Darryl F. Zanuck, who would eventually head Twentieth Century-Fox, turned out scripts for the canine star while employed as a writer at Warner Brothers.

6. Goldwyn was so proud of his taste in clothes that he never carried anything in his pockets, because he wanted nothing to detract from the perfect cut of his suit.

7. Alfred Hitchcock, at Selznick's invitation, came to Hollywood to make *Rebecca* for Selznick International in 1939. Released in 1940, it won the Oscar for Best Picture that year.

8. While all the movie moguls enjoyed testing the patience of those desiring to "take a meeting," MGM chief Irving Thalberg was known to keep people waiting outside his office for days at a time. The Marx Brothers once attempted to attract his attention by lighting a fire in the outer office.

9. Harry ("I don't have ulcers, I give them") Cohn. Not without a sense of humor, Cohn had an electric chair rigged up in Columbia's executive dining room. From a button on the floor, the studio chief could deliver a shock to his unsuspecting guest.

10. Samuel Goldwyn.

THERE'S NO BUSINESS LIKE

# AGENTS
## Sweetheart, Baby, That'll Be 15 Percent

1. Agent Jeff Berg, who represented many of the top writers and directors of the seventies, sold the rights to one novel for $2.15 million, the largest sum ever paid for the movie rights to a novel. What was its title?
    a) *Hawaii.*   c) *Airport.*   b) *The Island.*   d) *The Exorcist.*

2. What agent gained entry to show business as Louis B. Mayer's bootlegger in the 1920s?

3. This agent pioneered the "packaging" concept in Hollywood, combining literary properties with screenwriter, producer, director, and/or actors into one deal with a studio. Who was he?

4. An agent known for his abrasive manner as well as for his outstanding list of clients, he was the brother of a famous studio chief.

5. The Berg-Allenberg agency, which handled many of the top names in Hollywood in the forties, maintained what unique luxury item for its clients?

6. Greta Garbo's manager-agent Frank Edington was supposedly responsible for creating his client's aloof image. How did this come about?

7. Who was the first agent to arrange for his client to get a percentage of a film's profits?

8. This agent hastily took her client Clark Gable for two weeks of riding lessons at Griffith Park after telling a casting director, "Of course he can ride a horse!"

9. This Hollywood agent, who had once managed Al Jolson, had an affair with Marilyn Monroe and promoted her career enough to get her a first contract with Twentieth Century-Fox.

10. Why did Barbra Streisand fire ICM superagent Sue Mengers?

ANSWERS

# AGENTS
## Sweetheart, Baby, That'll Be 15 Percent

1  *The Island*, by Peter Benchley. The movie was a commercial flop.

2  Frank Orsatti. He became one of Mayer's closest friends, so when he formed his agency, his clients received preferential treatment at MGM. Some of his clients included Judy Garland, Edward G. Robinson, and Frank Capra.

3  Charles K. Feldman, whose Famous Artists agency formed the basis of the current giant, International Creative Management (ICM).

4  Myron Selznick, brother of David O. Selznick. His clients included Carole Lombard, Vivien Leigh, Pat O'Brien, and Katharine Hepburn.

5  It operated a 138-foot yacht for their use. Berg-Allenberg was later sold to the giant William Morris agency.

6  Garbo complained about being forced to pose for some ridiculous publicity shots upon her arrival in Hollywood, including one of her in gym shorts surrounded by the USC track team! Edington suggested that thereafter she simply play hard to get, so the studio played along and cultivated that image.

7  Lew Wasserman had Jimmy Stewart take less than his usual salary for *Bend of the River* (1952), in exchange for a percentage of the profits.

8  Minna Wallis, who was the sister of producer Hal Wallis.

9  Johnny Hyde.

10  Streisand had agreed—as a favor to Mengers—to appear in *All Night Long* (1981), a film by the agent's husband, director Jean-Claude Tramont. When Mengers took her usual 10 percent commission from Streisand's salary, Barbra became perturbed, since she had taken the job only as a personal favor. Sue gave back the money, but Barbra ended up firing her.

THERE'S NO BUSINESS LIKE

# LITERARY HOLLYWOOD
## Have Typewriter, Will Travel

1. What was unusual about William Faulkner's working arrangement with MGM?

2. The 1937 version of *A Star Is Born* was scripted in part by a writer much better known as a wit than as a dramatist. Who was she?

3. Which writer described working conditions at Columbia like this: "There's no fooling here. All the writers sit in cells in a row and the minute the typewriter stops someone pokes his head in the door to see if you are thinking. Otherwise, it's like the hotel business."
   a) Dashiell Hammett.  b) S. J. Perelman.  c) Nathanael West.
   d) Neil Simon.

4. This legendary American novelist polished dialogue in the screenplay for *Gone With the Wind* (1939), but did not receive a screen credit. Who was he?

5. Unlike most of the "serious" writers who came to Hollywood strictly for the money, this novelist and film critic was drawn to screenwriting by a love of film and an admiration for director John Huston. Who was he?

6. While visiting Hollywood in 1932, this literary giant refused a $50,000 offer to work for MGM, but found time for a brief dalliance with Jean Harlow.

7. A Nobel Prize–winning author consistently refused to work on the film adaptations of his novels, describing the best way for a writer to deal with Hollywood as follows: "You throw them your book, they throw you the money, then you jump into your car and drive like hell back the way you came." Who was the writer?

8. What Pulitzer Prize–winning playwright also won an Academy Award nomination for his acting?

9. The great mystery writer Raymond Chandler adapted a James M. Cain novel into a 1944 film that starred a man who would later become one of TV's most famous fathers. What was the film's title?

10. Which of the following writers did *not* work on a screenplay for an Alfred Hitchcock film:
    a) William Faulkner.  b) Raymond Chandler.
    c) Thornton Wilder.  d) Dorothy Parker.  e) Maxwell Anderson.

ANSWERS

# LITERARY HOLLYWOOD
## Have Typewriter, Will Travel

1   Faulkner had an understanding with director Howard Hawks that he could work at home if he wanted to. Working at home was not unusual, but when the studio attempted to contact the writer at his Hollywood apartment, they discovered that "home" meant Oxford, Mississippi.

2   Dorothy Parker, who was probably more famous for remarks like, "One more drink and I'll be under the host!" *A Star Is Born* was remade in 1954 and again in 1976.

3   Nathanael West hammered out two complete screenplays for Columbia in a seven-week period for a salary of just $350 per week. He later described the seedy side of Hollywood in his novel, *The Day of the Locust*, which was made into a film in 1975.

4   F. Scott Fitzgerald. Between 1937 and 1940 Fitzgerald worked on fifteen different screenplays, but received screen credit for only one: *Three Comrades* (1938).

5   James Agee, author of *A Death in the Family*, quit his concurrent jobs as film critic for both *Time* and *The Nation* to write for the movies. He collaborated most successfully with Huston on *The African Queen* (1951).

6   Thomas Wolfe spent a little time with Harlow before going home again.

7   Ernest Hemingway, whose screenplay for *The Old Man and the Sea* (1958) was the only one of the many movie versions of his novels on which he agreed to work. His basic complaint about screenwriting was: "All you think about is pictures, when you ought to be thinking about people."

8   Sam Shepard, whose play *Buried Child* won the Pulitzer in 1979, and who was nominated for an Oscar for his performance in *The Right Stuff* (1984).

9   *Double Indemnity* (1944) starred Fred MacMurray, who was later known as the father of TV's "My Three Sons."

10  Faulkner did not. The others' credits include: *Strangers on a Train* (Chandler, 1951); *Shadow of a Doubt* (Wilder, 1943); *Saboteur* (Parker, 1942); and *The Wrong Man* (Anderson, 1957).

THERE'S NO BUSINESS LIKE

# PRODUCERS
## The Ones Who Put It All Together

1. This actress was the producer of a 1981 adventure film she starred in for her company, Svengali Productions.

2. MGM producer Harry Rapf was known as "Mayer's Sundial." Why?

3. Walter Wanger was producer of the famous $44 million remake of *Cleopatra* (1963), but was involved in an even more embarrassing experience in 1951. What happened?

4. This producer made his reputation—and his fortune—by becoming one of Hollywood's major foreign film importers, scoring his first great financial success in 1959 with the Italian-made *Hercules*.

5. He began directing his own films in 1955 after having established a reputation as a producer of "socially conscious" films such as *Home of the Brave* (1949), *The Men* (1950), and the supposedly allegorical film about McCarthyism, *High Noon* (1952).

6. This MGM producer, who has a special Oscar named for him, was known to insist on the endless re-editing and reshooting of a film until it met with his satisfaction.

7. This producer, who has a reputation as a "glamour maker," is credited with changing the images (and thereby boosting the careers) of Doris Day, Lana Turner, and Jacqueline Bisset.

8. In 1968 a young, unknown producer-director made a documentary called *Filmmaker* about the making of the first movie by another young, unknown producer-director. Both would go on to spectacular success in later years. Who were they?

9. Name the flamboyant movie producer who produced only one film, *Around the World in 80 Days* (1956).

10. Name the production company, founded in 1954 by James Nicholson and Samuel Arkoff, that churned out low-budget movies aimed at the teenage market.

ANSWERS

# PRODUCERS
## The Ones Who Put It All Together

1.  Bo Derek produced and starred in *Tarzan, The Ape Man*.

2.  Because of the shape of his large, protruding nose.

3.  He shot wife Joan Bennett's agent, Jennings Lang, and served three months in prison.

4.  Joseph E. Levine, who also financed the Italian films *8½* (1963) and *Two Women* (1961), in addition to personally producing *The Carpetbaggers* (1963).

5.  Stanley Kramer later continued this trend as a director with *Judgment at Nuremberg* (1961) and *Guess Who's Coming to Dinner* (1967), among others.

6.  Irving Thalberg.

7.  Ross Hunter, producer of *Pillow Talk* (1959), *Imitation of Life* (1959), and *Airport* (1969).

8.  George Lucas made this film about the making of Francis Ford Coppola's *The Rain People* (1969).

9.  Mike Todd, who many thought to be one of the greatest con men of all time. He made a career of spending other people's money. Using his charm he convinced many top stars to make cameo appearances in his epic film.

10. American International Pictures (AIP), which produced *I Was a Teenage Werewolf* (1957), *Beach Blanket Bingo* (1965), and *The Wild Angels* (1966), to name only a few.

THERE'S NO BUSINESS LIKE

# DIRECTORS
## Quiet on the Set!

1. He was known as a "woman's director" to the point that some male stars were uncomfortable starring in his films for fear of being upstaged by their leading ladies.

2. Why did director Roman Polanski flee the United States for Paris in early 1978?

3. Steven Spielberg directed one made-for-TV movie in his career. It was first run on ABC in 1971. What was it called?

4. Director Michael Curtiz, whose long career began as an actor in pre–World War I Budapest, is probably best known for *Casablanca* (1942), but also made a significant contribution to the careers of both James Cagney and Joan Crawford. How?

5. Howard Hawks was successful directing virtually every genre of movie in his long career. Which of the following films did he *not* direct?
   a) *Scarface* (1932).  b) *The Big Sleep* (1946).
   c) *Gentlemen Prefer Blondes* (1953).  d) *Rio Bravo* (1959).
   e) *Land of the Pharaohs* (1955).  f) *Red Line 7000* (1965).

6. This director was nominated for several Emmy Awards for his TV work with shows such as "Chrysler Theater," "Ben Casey," and "The Naked City" before turning to feature films, where he has directed good friend Robert Redford a number of times.

7. John Huston's spectacular career has spanned five decades with no diminishment of talent, as his 1985 *Prizzi's Honor* showed. But even the very *first* film he directed became an all-time great. What was it?

8. Martin Scorsese, whose films include *Mean Streets* (1973), *Alice Doesn't Live Here Anymore* (1974), *Taxi Driver* (1976), *New York, New York* (1977), and *Body Double* (1984), as a boy in New York aspired to another life's work. What was it?

9. Since the beginning of his Hollywood career in the 1940s, this remarkably successful director has never directed a film written by anyone other than himself (and various collaborators).

10. Why did director John Ford wear the same shirt every day while filming *Mary of Scotland* (1936)?

ANSWERS

# DIRECTORS
## Quiet on the Set!

1. George Cukor directed Garbo in *Camille* (1936), Ingrid Bergman in *Gaslight* (1944), Judy Holliday in *Born Yesterday* (1950), and Judy Garland in *A Star Is Born* (1954), as well as a good portion (uncredited) of *Gone With the Wind* (1939).

2. He was about to be sentenced in a statutory rape case involving a thirteen-year-old girl. Hollywood's joke at the time was that his next film would be called "Close Encounters of the Third Grade."

3. *Duel*, which starred Dennis Weaver as a driver being relentlessly pursued by a monstrous truck—sort of a *Jaws* on wheels.

4. He directed them to their only Oscars: Cagney in *Yankee Doodle Dandy* (1942) and Crawford in *Mildred Pierce* (1945).

5. Hawks directed *all* of the above.

6. Sydney Pollack, whose movie credits include *They Shoot Horses, Don't They?* (1969), *The Way We Were* (1973), *Three Days of the Condor* (1975), and *Tootsie* (1983).

7. *The Maltese Falcon* (1941) marked Huston's auspicious debut as a director. He had been under contract to Warner Brothers as a writer and told them he would agree to renew his option only if they would let him direct.

8. He wanted to be a priest, and attended a preparatory seminary until academic and disciplinary problems forced him to leave.

9. Billy Wilder, whose director-screenwriter credits include *Double Indemnity* (1944), *Sunset Boulevard* (1950), and *Some Like It Hot* (1959), as well as many of the most successful Jack Lemmon–Walter Matthau comedies.

10. The superstitious Ford wore the shirt while directing the hit movie *The Informer* (1935), and he hoped he'd have the same good luck with *Mary of Scotland*. Unfortunately, the movie bombed.

THERE'S NO BUSINESS LIKE

# HOLLYWOOD AND THE LAW
## Torts and Trials in Tinsel Town

1. Jerry Geisler was for years one of the most sought-after men in Hollywood, though he never worked on a movie. Who was he?

2. Why did fashion designer Orry-Kelly have to borrow a stuffed dove from a Louisiana museum for a hat Bette Davis wore in *The Little Foxes* (1941)?

3. This actor became a part of legal history when his ex-live-in mate successfully sued him for a property settlement after their six-year affair.

4. After 1942, the expression "in like Flynn" took on a particularly unpleasant meaning for Errol Flynn. Why?

5. This leading man was convicted for possession of marijuana and sentenced to a sixty-day prison term in Hollywood's biggest scandal of 1948.

6. The Rex was a popular gambling spot with the Hollywood crowd in the thirties and was often advertised openly as such. Why were they able to do this?

7. Name the 1907 movie, based on a Lew Wallace novel of the same title, that established an important legal precedent.

8. Name the actress who was an advocate for liberalizing adoption laws in California for single parents.

9. When Dyan Cannon sued Cary Grant for divorce, she mentioned his abuse of this substance during the proceedings.

10. In 1954 Kirk Douglas sued Walt Disney for invasion of privacy. What were the details of the suit?

ANSWERS

# HOLLYWOOD AND THE LAW
## Torts and Trials in Tinsel Town

1  Probably the most famous lawyer in the film community, handling celebrity cases that ranged from divorces and nightclub brawls, to the successful defense of Errol Flynn in his statutory rape case.

2  Because conservation laws in California forbade the use of stuffed fowl on hats.

3  Lee Marvin, father of "palimony."

4  The phrase became a smirking reference to his trial on charges of statutory rape. Although acquitted, he did not live down the stigma.

5  Robert Mitchum.

6  Because the *Rex* was a ship anchored off Santa Monica. It featured dancing and entertainment as well as various forms of gambling, but was forced to close in 1939, after pressure from state attorney general Earl Warren.

7  *Ben Hur*. The judgment established certain author's rights with regards to material made into films. The Kalem Company was forced to pay $25,000 in damages for copyright infringements.

8  Joan Crawford, who as a single person had adopted four children: Christina, Christopher, Cathy, and Cynthia. She wanted the California laws changed so that a single person could adopt a child in the state.

9  LSD. When Grant took the substance it was legal and he was under medical supervision. The actor claimed he was using the drug because he was looking for the real truth.

10  The Douglas family, while guests at Disney's home, were filmed for "home movies" riding Disney's train in the producer's backyard. The film later showed up plugging a TV special. Douglas sued, having never agreed to let Disney use the film for promotional purposes.

THERE'S NO BUSINESS LIKE

# FLOPS AND OTHER BOO-BOOS

1. In spite of eleven Academy Award nominations, this 1960 John Wayne production managed to lose millions at the box office.

2. A former stage and screen actress, she first began writing about Hollywood at age fifty and achieved much greater success than she did in front of the cameras.

3. What was the reason for the garish color changes throughout the movie *South Pacific* (1958)?

4. A record $9.5 million was paid for the movie rights to this smash Broadway musical, which was turned into *the* Hollywood box-office disaster of 1982.

5. Steven Spielberg's most unsuccessful film reportedly lost about $20 million. What was its title?

6. What was the only James Bond movie that lost money?

7. This Francis Ford Coppola film is credited with bringing about the downfall of his Zoetrope Studios.

8. Accounting for inflation, what was the most expensive movie ever made?

9. In her brief career as a Hollywood columnist she once took Joan Crawford to task for combing her hair in public.

10. Shortly after completing work on the phenomenally popular film that marked his Hollywood debut in 1967, he went back to collecting unemployment compensation because he had squandered his $17,000 salary.

ANSWERS

# FLOPS AND OTHER BOO-BOOS

1. *The Alamo*, which the Duke produced, directed, and starred in, took in only half of its $15 million cost.

2. Hedda Hopper.

3. Director Joshua Logan wanted to capture the visual effect of the stage version of the story, in which the stage changed color during every song. Tinted filters were used on the camera lens, creating a less-than-desirable effect.

4. *Annie* cost $42 million to make and reportedly needed to gross $150 million just to break even. At last count it was only halfway there.

5. *1941* (1979), his big-budget comedy that starred John Belushi. Yes, everyone makes mistakes.

6. *Casino Royale* (1967), which starred such un-Bond-like people as David Niven, Peter Sellers, and Woody Allen.

7. *One from the Heart* (1982) cost $26 million and grossed less than $1 million in its first year, causing Coppola to suffer a very personal financial disaster.

8. *Cleopatra* (1963) cost $44 million when it was made, the equivalent of about $110.6 million in 1980s dollars. It achieved a net loss equaling 46.2 million modern dollars.

9. Dorothy Kilgallen. With juicy tidbits like that, it's no wonder Dorothy went back to New York.

10. Dustin Hoffman, who has not collected unemployment since the release of *The Graduate*.

THERE'S NO BUSINESS LIKE

# IT'S NOT IN MY CONTRACT

1  What actress had a contract that banned her from the studio commissary?

2  W. C. Fields's contract with the Mack Sennett studio had an unusual clause about the method of payment. What was it?

3  This actress had a clause written into her 1955 studio contract that stated that all her films had to be in color.

4  When Howard Hughes hired Ben Hecht to write the screenplay for the movie *Scarface* (1932), what unusual condition did Hecht insist upon in his contract?

5  Which of W. C. Fields's co-stars made it part of her contract agreement that W. C. had to refrain from drinking on the set?

6  Paul Muni once requested a waiver of the provision in his contract that he get sole star billing above the title. What prompted this unusual gesture?

7  What actor's contract guaranteed he would work only a nine-to-five day on the set?

8  What fine-print clause did Joan Crawford have in her contract to insure she would be comfortable while working on the set?

9  One of the last contract stars of the studio era in Hollywood had a clause providing that she would not have to work during the first two days of her period. Who?

10  This actress trusted Louis B. Mayer so much that she never had a written contract: when they made a film together it was by verbal agreement.

ANSWERS

# IT'S NOT IN MY CONTRACT

1   Shirley Temple. Her mother insisted that, except on her birthday, she not be allowed in the Fox commissary, to avoid her being "petted and pampered."

2   It specified that Fields's $5,000 per week salary be paid on two days: $2,500 on Monday and $2,500 on Wednesday.

3   Marilyn Monroe.

4   Hecht demanded that he be paid $1,000 at the end of each working day. That way, Hecht reasoned, he would have only wasted one working day if Hughes was insolvent.

5   Mae West insisted on this arrangement when working with him on *My Little Chickadee* (1940).

6   When making *Juarez* (1949), Muni felt that co-star Bette Davis deserved equal billing.

7   Clark Gable. His contract with Metro also specified he would only fly in planes with more than two engines.

8   Crawford was guaranteed that the temperature on her set would be maintained at a chilly 58 degrees F.

9   Elizabeth Taylor.

10  Katharine Hepburn

THERE'S NO BUSINESS LIKE

# GREASEPAINT AND LIP GLOSS
## Makeup

1. Actors in this movie wore fifty-pound masks that combined human and animal features in a way that allowed the human personalities to express emotion in spite of the highly realistic makeup.

2. When Marlon Brando disguised himself for this movie role as a Mexican revolutionary, many critics thought his makeup made him look Oriental. Who was Brando attempting to look like?

3. What was it about Tyrone Power's face that caused Darryl Zanuck to remark, "He looks like a monkey," when the mogul saw the actor's screen test?

4. Who created the makeup for Boris Karloff's Frankenstein?

5. Name the Hollywood makeup master who invented false eyelashes, lip gloss, and pancake makeup.

6. Shortly before his death in 1930, he wrote the official entry for the *Encyclopedia Britannica* on makeup.

7. Percy Westmore was the first to style this star's hair in bangs, a style she affects to this day. Who is the star?

8. Lon Chaney was famous for creating his own makeup in horror film classics, but who did the makeup for James Cagney when he starred as Chaney in *Man of a Thousand Faces* (1957)?

9. Why did Chinese-American actor Keye Luke lose his job in the movie *Dragon Seed* (1944)?

10. Name the 1941 horror film classic in which Spencer Tracy refused to wear makeup to alter his appearance.

ANSWERS

# GREASEPAINT AND LIP GLOSS
## Makeup

1. *Planet of the Apes* (1968). After ape features were drawn on photographs of the actors, they were sculpted in clay onto a mask of each actor's face, and the final mask molds were made from these models.

2. Emiliano Zapata for the 1952 film *Viva Zapata*. Brando's makeup actually duplicated Diego Rivera's portrait of the revolutionary.

3. Power's bushy eyebrows made him look like a stand-in for Bonzo. Makeup man Ray Sebastian used a plucker with an airhose attachment to remove the offending hairs.

4. Jack Pierce. In doing research for the film, he discovered that there are various ways a surgeon can cut a skull. Pierce chose the simplest method to simulate, which is the cutting off the top of the skull.

5. Max Factor. In 1914 Factor created the first motion-picture makeup—sanitary greasepaint in a tube. Prior to Factor's creation, greasepaint came only in stick form and photographed too heavy.

6. Lon Chaney. He created makeup for all his movie roles. Two of the most memorable were *The Phantom of the Opera* (1925) and *The Hunchback of Notre Dame* (1923). In the same way that a great magician protects the tricks of his trade, Chaney took many of his makeup secrets to the grave.

7. Claudette Colbert.

8. Bud Westmore and Jack Kevan.

9. Reputedly Luke made Katharine Hepburn's attempt at looking Chinese for the movie an obvious fake. The contrast was very marked, with the very Caucasian Hepburn playing opposite the Chinese actor.

10. *Dr. Jekyll and Mr. Hyde* (1941). Tracy used his acting prowess rather than makeup technique to change him from the kindly Dr. Jekyll to the sinister Mr. Hyde.

THERE'S NO BUSINESS LIKE

# COSTUMES
# Furs, Feathers, and Finery

1. The Western Costume Company, reputedly the largest such business in the world, started out in 1912 as a dealer in American Indian gear. How did they get into the movies?

2. Name the Warner Brothers head designer of the thirties who got his hyphenated name as a result of a typing error in his first contract.

3. Why did designer Walter Plunkett have a bolt of green velvet fabric deliberately faded to make a dress for a famous scene in a Hollywood classic?

4. Robert Redford's impeccable wardrobe for his portrayal of Jay Gatsby was designed by a person not usually thought of in connection with film. Who was he?

5. The hats designed by Cecil Beaton for this movie production were so large, Warner Brothers used an army surplus quonset hut as a dressing room.

6. Name the designer who quit the movie business when Louis B. Mayer insisted he create down-to-earth fashions for Greta Garbo.

7. This invention resulted because stars were fearful of wrinkling their costumes between takes on the set.

8. This Hollywood designer got her first job at Paramount by answering an ad in the *Los Angeles Times* for an artist.

9. Helen Rose won an Academy Award in 1966 for costume design in black and white. The award was an acknowledgement of Rose's artistry in padding this glamorous actress's hips and cleverly cutting her clothes to make her look frumpy. Name the film and the actress.

10. In 1934 this Hollywood law had a direct impact on necklines of female stars in movies. What was this censorship move called?

ANSWERS

# COSTUMES
## Furs, Feathers, and Finery

1  The shop's proprietor happened to comment to cowboy star William S. Hart that the costumes of the Indians in his recent movie were not authentic. Soon after, Western was supplying these and most other early movie costumes.

2  Orry-Kelly (John Orry Kelly) thought the hyphen gave him an air of class, so he kept it. The veteran designer dressed Bette Davis and Ava Gardner for the films.

3  He faded the velvet so it would appear the dress had been made from the dining-room curtains in the plantation house of Tara. Scarlett O'Hara wore the dress in the all-time great movie *Gone With the Wind* (1939).

4  Ralph Lauren.

*My Fair Lady* (1964). The hats in question were seen in profusion in the famous Ascot scene.

6  Adrian, who started his career making costumes for Rudolph Valentino in the 1920s, couldn't take Mayer's constant interference on the 1941 movie *Two-Faced Woman*.

7  The "leaning board," a padded wooden plank with armrests and footrests angled so the stars could relax on the set without doing damage to their costumes.

8  Edith Head. She had no formal training as a dress designer and borrowed sketches from her art-school classmates to apply for the job. Her career was remarkable and she won eight Oscars for her work in films.

9  *Who's Afraid of Virginia Woolf?* (1966), starring Elizabeth Taylor.

10  The Anti-Cleavage Law of 1934.

## DEFINITIONS
## What Does It All Mean?

1. What was the "running W"?

2. What was the coloring process called Technicolor named for?

3. What do you call the slate that is photographed at the start of each shot that has relevant information written on it such as shot and take numbers?

4. The color standard used by all film labs in the United States is called:
    a) Specturn.   b) Hues-are-us.   c) Rainbow reading.   d) China girl.

5. What is meant by the term CinemaScope?

6. What is a cattle call?

7. A key grip does not open the studio doors in the morning. What does a key grip do?

8. What is the screen-credit term for the chief electrician who is responsible for the lighting equipment?

9. Why did Alan Ladd need an "apple box," while Gary Cooper did not?

10. We've all heard the term executive producer, but what does an executive producer do?

# ANSWERS
# DEFINITIONS
## What Does It All Mean?

1. It was a trip wire used to make horses fall over at the critical moment during filming. The cruel device, which broke countless horses' legs and necks, has since been outlawed.

2. The name honors the Massachusetts Institute of Technology (MIT), probably because it was developed by MIT alumnus Dr. Herbert Thomas Kalmus.

3. A clapboard. Fastened to the top of the clapboard are clapsticks that are slapped together to cue the soundtrack.

4. China girl. The negative film image used for the standard is that of a Caucasian girl's face.

5. CinemaScope was invented in 1913 by a French optics professor named Henri Chrétien. He invented the first anamorphic lens, which compresses horizontally a very wide image onto a standard 35mm frame.

6. An audition for the minor roles in a production. Cecil B. DeMille's casts of thousands were recruited at cattle calls.

7. A key grip is the stagehand on a movie set who is in charge of the other stagehands.

8. Gaffer.

9. An apple box is a wooden box on which a person or thing can stand to increase height.

10. The executive producer handles the financial aspects of the movie production. Sometimes the executive producer is involved with the creative element of the film and sometimes not.

THERE'S NO BUSINESS LIKE

# IT'S ONLY MONEY

1. What was the House of Francis?

2. Yul Brynner received the then-staggering sum of $1 million for his role in *Solomon and Sheba* (1958). Why did he have such great bargaining power?

3. This Beverly Hills restaurant is so exclusive that its telephone number is unlisted.

4. What was the most expensive black-and-white movie ever made?

5. Known simply as Ocean House, this unbelievably luxurious Santa Monica mansion had fifty-five bathrooms, thirty-seven fireplaces, and thirty-two servants. Who did it belong to?

6. This 1933 film is credited with saving Paramount from bankruptcy.

7. It took four years to build the sixteen-acre, forty-four-room Italian Renaissance estate called Greenacres. Who was the actor who owned this Beverly Hills palace?

8. Name the wealthy community about a mile west of Beverly Hills that, when first developed in 1922, would not sell property to movie people.

9. Name the actress who kept her jewels in the refrigerator for safekeeping.

10. Katharine Hepburn owned the rights to this play and sold them to MGM for $250,000.

ANSWERS

# IT'S ONLY MONEY

1. A house of prostitution frequented by Errol Flynn and other well-known Hollywood stars. Its famous madame, Lee Francis, was arrested only once in the more than thirty years she was in business.

2. The producers of the film were somewhat desperate; filming had already begun with Tyrone Power, who inconveniently died well into the picture. Since Power had already done a number of close-ups, they could not use a double and simply had to reshoot most of the film with Brynner.

3. Ma Maison.

4. *Who's Afraid of Virginia Woolf?* (1966) cost $7.5 million—thanks largely to the salaries of its stars, Liz Taylor and Richard Burton.

5. Marion Davies, paramour of William Randolph Hearst and one of Hollywood's wealthiest stars.

6. *She Done Him Wrong*, the Mae West comedy that grossed more than $2 million in the United States alone.

7. Harold Lloyd. The cost of keeping the estate was too much for Lloyd's heirs and the home was leveled in 1975 to make way for apartment buildings.

8. Bel Air. Developer Alfonso Bell did not want Hollywood types in his exclusive community. He changed his mind when the Great Depression hit and the dreaded movie people were the only ones who could afford his expensive land.

9. Norma Talmadge. In the early twenties insurance companies considered movie people a poor risk, so in lieu of insurance, Ms. Talmadge kept her valuables in the vegetable bin.

10. *The Philadelphia Story* (1940). After being labeled "box-office poison" in 1938 by the Independent Theater Owners of America, Hepburn made her comeback in this 1940 comedy.

THERE'S NO BUSINESS LIKE

# NUMBERS . . . NUMBERS . . . NUMBERS

1   This 1958 movie spectacular featured fifty stars and 68,894 extras in thirteen countries wearing 74,685 costumes.

2   If inflation is taken into account, what is the top money-making film of all time?

3   In 1948 Howard Hughes bought it for $9.50 per share for a total of $8,825,500. What was it that Hughes purchased?

4   David O. Selznick was required to pay a $5,000 fine for violating the Production Code, but after a hard battle with the censors was allowed to keep this highly controversial line of dialogue in his great 1939 film.

5   When she was discovered by Howard Hughes, she was a ten-dollar-a-week receptionist in a chiropodist's office.

6   In the 1940 movie *You're in the Army Now*, it lasted 185 seconds. What was it?

7   When Burt Reynolds played football at Florida State University, he wore the same number on his jersey that he wore in the movie *The Longest Yard* (1974) What was the number?

8   This bad guy with the aristocratic-sounding voice stood only five feet seven inches, and in one film played some scenes with Ingrid Bergman while standing on a ramp.

9   Match Liz Taylor's husbands with the years of their weddings:
    Nicky Hilton.              1957.
    Michael Wilding.           1976.
    Mike Todd.                 1950.
    Eddie Fisher.              1975.
    Richard Burton (first).    1959.
    Richard Burton (second).   1952.
    John Warner.               1964.

10  Her mother had forewarned her about boarding flight number three, from Indianapolis to Burbank, California, on January 16, 1942.

ANSWERS

# NUMBERS...NUMBERS...NUMBERS

1   *Around the World in 80 Days.*

2   When the value of the 1939 dollar is considered, *Gone With the Wind* is the all-time champ. The average movie ticket at the time cost twenty-three cents.

3   Hughes bought controlling interest in RKO studios from Floyd Odlum.

4   "Frankly, my dear, I don't give a damn" shocked audiences in *Gone With the Wind*. The Catholic Legion of Decency gave the movie a B rating: "morally objectionable in part for all."

5   Jane Russell, who was hired as the sexy female star of *The Outlaw* (1943).

6   The longest kiss in screen history. The lingering lips belonged to Regis Toomey and Jane Wyman.

7   Number 22.

8   Claude Rains was a villain-on-a-ramp in *Notorious* (1946) and also created memorable scoundrels in *Anthony Adverse* (1936), *Casablanca* (1942), and *Mr. Smith Goes to Washington* (1939), to name a few.

9   Nicky Hilton, 1950; Michael Wilding, 1952; Mike Todd, 1957; Eddie Fisher, 1959; Richard Burton (first), 1964; Richard Burton (second), 1975; John Warner, 1976.

10  Carole Lombard and her mother both died when their flight crashed. Her mother, a believer in numerology and astrology, predicted that the flight would be ill-fated.

THERE'S NO BUSINESS LIKE

# FIRSTS

1  What was the first movie to be filmed in Technicolor?

2  The first full-length X-rated cartoon feature was based on a famous underground comic-book character. What was his (and the film's) name?

3  What was the first movie to gross over $100 million?

4  After a difficult battle with the censors, what 1966 movie was released as the first Hollywood film to earn an SMA (Suggested for Mature Audiences) rating?

5  The first movie actress to appear on the cover of *People* magazine appeared on its very first issue in March 1974. Who was she?

6  Name the silent-film director who reputedly invented the casting couch.

7  The first movie shot in CinemaScope was:
   a) *The Robe* (1953).   b) *Ben Hur* (1959).
   c) *Gone With the Wind* (1939).
   d) *The Ten Commandments* (1956).

8  Name the 1922 film shot on location by Robert Flaherty that depicts the daily life of the Eskimos.

9  Name the two female leads that received an Oscar nomination for Best Actress in the 1950 film *All About Eve*.

10 In the Jean Harlow movie *Goldie* (1931), this word was used for the first time on the silver screen.

ANSWERS

# FIRSTS

1. *Becky Sharp* (1934).

2. *Fritz The Cat* (1972), a creation of cartoonist R. Crumb.

3. *Jaws* (1975).

4. *Who's Afraid of Virginia Woolf?*, which starred Liz Taylor and Richard Burton, was released with the stipulation that "no one under eighteen will be admitted unless accompanied by a parent." The British-made *Georgy Girl* (also 1966) was the very first SMA film distributed in the U.S.

5. Mia Farrow.

6. Mack Sennett.

7. *The Robe* was the first CinemaScope film. At the time the movie industry was in a slump because audiences were more interested in a new diversion, television. Spyros Skouras, chairman of Twentieth Century-Fox, mortgaged the entire studio on the gamble that CinemaScope would hit big at the box office. It did and saved the company.

8. *Nanook of the North* was a revolutionary type of film, the first documentary. The movie chronicled the lives of the Eskimos through the story of one man and his family.

9. Anne Baxter and Bette Davis. The fact that two women from the same movie were nominated for the honor was a Hollywood first.

10. Tramp, to refer to a woman of loose morals.

# INDEX

Abraham, F. Murray, 62–63
Academy Awards, 10–11, 14–15, 20–21, 22–23, 24–25, 40–49, 54–55, 66–67, 72–73, 106–07, 108–09, 110–11, 114–15, 116–17, 124–25, 140–41, 142–43, 146–47, 158–59, 168–69, 176–77, 180–81
Ackerman, Forrest J., 166–67
Adrian, Gilbert, 46–47, 110–11, 152–53, 194–95
Agar, John, 2–3
Agee, James, 180–81
Aherne, Brian, 46–47
Aldrich, Robert, 52–53
Ali, Mohammed, 96–97
Allen, Woody, 8–9, 42–43, 90–91, 188–89
Ambassador Hotel, 138–39
American International Pictures, 182–83
Anderson, Maxwell, 180–81
Andrews, Julie, 114–15, 140–41
Andrews, Reverend George Reid, 74–75
Angeli, Pier, 30–31
Anka, Paul, 62–63
Arbuckle, Roscoe "Fatty", 58–59
Arce, Hector, 96–97
Arden, Eve, 100–01
Arkoff, Samuel, 182–83
Astaire, Fred, 54–55, 62–63, 98–99, 160–61
Astor, Mary, 30–31
Atkinson, Lynn, 18–19
Autry, Gene, 132–33
Aykroyd, Dan, 100–01
Ayres, Lew, 48–49, 148–49

Bacall, Lauren, 14–15, 26–27, 30–31, 62–63, 84–85, 104–05, 174–75
Bacharach, Burt, 44–45
Bacon, James, 2–3, 86–87
Baker, Mary, 104–05
Balfe, Veronica, 58–59
Ball, Lucille, 118–19
Bancroft, Anne, 40–41, 82–83, 92–93
Bankhead, Tallulah, 162–63
Bara, Theda, 164–65
Barrett, Rona, 80–81
Barrymore, John, 60–61, 90–91, 122–23, 142–43, 166–67
Barrymore, John, Jr., 12–13
Barton, Reverend William, 74–75
Baum, L. Frank, 134–35
Baxter, Anne, 22–23, 202–03
Beaton, Cecil, 194–95

Beatty, Warren, 44–45, 90–91, 150–51
Beery, Wallace, 40–41, 168–69
Bell, Alfonso, 198–99
Belushi, John, 100–01, 144–45, 188–89
Benchley, Robert, 48–49, 58–59, 138–39, 178–79
Bennett, Joan, 182–83
Benny, Jack, 100–01, 144–45
Berg, Jeff, 178–79
Berg-Allenberg Agency, 178–79
Bergen, Candice, 22–23
Bergman, Ingrid, 98–99, 184–85, 200–01
Berlin, Irving, 62–63
Berman, Pandro S., 130–31
Bern, Paul, 164–65
Bernardi, Herschel, 42–43
Bernstein, Walter, 42–43
Berry, Ken, 158–59
Besser, Joe, 24–25
Bessie, Alvah, 42–43
Beverly Hills Hotel, 2–3, 142–43, 148–49, 160–61
Beverly Wilshire Hotel, 150–51
Biberman, Herbert, 42–43
Bill Haley and the Comets, 12–13
Biltmore Hotel, 142–43
Biograph Studios, 36–37
Bisset, Jacqueline, 182–83
Black, Charles, 94–95
Blair, Linda, 70–71, 100–01
Blake, Arthur, 60–61
Blane, Sally, 66–67
Bogart, Humphrey, 10–11, 26–27, 50–51, 82–83, 104–05, 146–47
Bogdanovich, Peter, 22–23, 92–93
Bolger, Ray, 134–35
Bondurant, Bob, 166–67
Boone, Debbie, 40–41
Boorman, John, 96–97
Borden, Olive, 160–61
Borge, Victor, 100–01
Borgnine, Ernest, 172–73
Bow, Clara, 38–39, 58–59, 174–75
Boyer, Charles, 90–91
Brando, Jocelyn, 4–5
Brando, Marlon, 4–5, 8–9, 10–11, 44–45, 50–51, 66–67, 72–73, 98–99, 106–07, 126–27, 162–63, 192–93
Breen, Joe, 26–27
Brennan, Walter, 88–89, 168–69
Briggs, Joe Bob, 92–93
Brisson, Frederick, 30–31
Bromfield, Louis, 104–05
Bronson, Charles, 50–51, 168–69
Brooks, Clarence, 54–55
Brooks, Mel, 172–73

**205**

Brown, C.C., 152–53
Brown Derby, 138–39, 146–47, 148–49, 158–59
Browning, Tod, 64–65
Brynner, Yul, 168–69, 198–99
Bullock's, 142–43
Burns, George, 144–45
Burstyn, Ellen, 168–69
Burton, Richard, 14–15, 28–29, 66–67, 100–01, 130–31, 152–53, 198–99, 200–01, 202–03
Butterfield's, 142–43
Byron, Lord Alfred, 92–93

Caan, James, 70–71, 168–69
Caesar, Sid, 172–73
Cafe Gala, The, 148–49
Cagney, James, 8–9, 46–47, 50–51, 96–97, 184–85, 192–93
Cain, James M., 180–81
Cambridge, Godfrey, 54–55
Cannon, Dyan, 186–87
Capote, Truman, 32–33, 88–89
Capra, Frank, 44–45, 48–49, 66–67, 108–09, 116–17, 178–79
Carmichael, Hoagy, 62–63
Carol, Sue, 82–83
Caron, Leslie, 62–63
Carpenter, John, 64–65
Carson, Johnny, 76–77
Carter, Jimmy, 52–53
Cassini, Oleg, 52–53
Castle, William, 64–65
Catalina Island, 74–75
Catholic Legion of Decency, 200–01
Cavett, Dick, 122–23
Central Casting, 56–57
Chan, Charlie, 4–5
Chandler, Norman, 156–57
Chandler, Raymond, 28–29, 180–81
Chaney, Lon, 64–65, 192–93
Chaney, Lon, Jr., 84–85, 156–57
Chaplin, Charlie, 2–3, 30–31, 36–37, 38–39, 40–41, 118–19, 144–45, 148–49, 150–51, 176–77
Chaplin, Charles, Jr., 12–13
Charisse, Cyd, 62–63
Chase, Chevy, 120–21
Chasen, Dave, 148–49
Chateau Marmont Hotel, 144–45
Chayefsky, Paddy, 140–41, 172–73
Chessman, Caryl, 50–51
Chretién, Henri, 196–97
Church of the Good Shepherd, 142–43
Cimino, Michael, 74–75
CinemaScope, 196–97, 202–03

Ciro's, 138–39
Cisco Kid, 4–5
Clark, Mae, 8–9, 84–85
Clift, Montgomery, 4–5, 130–31
Clive, Colin, 84–85
Club Alabam, 144–45
Clune's Auditorium, 142–43
Cochran, Eddie, 12–13
Cock 'n' Bull, 138–39
Cocoanut Grove, 138–39
Cohn, Harry, 2–3, 86–87, 108–09, 126–27, 164–65, 168–69, 176–77
Colbert, Claudette, 14–15, 58–59, 66–67, 160–61, 192–93
Cole, Lester, 42–43
Cole, Nat King, 144–45
Coleman, Herbert, 174–75
Collingwood, Charles, 18–19
Collins, Joan, 16–17, 74–75
Colman, Ronald, 54–55, 160–61
Colony Club, 138–39
Columbia Pictures, 108–09, 164–65, 176–77, 180–81
Comedy Store, 138–39
Connery, Sean, 114–15
Coogan, Jackie, 20–21
Cooper, Gary, 4–5, 16–17, 24–25, 58–59, 60–61, 62–63, 86–87, 88–89, 96–97, 116–17, 156–57, 174–75, 196–97
Cooper, Jackie, 20–21, 86–87
Coppola, Carmine, 22–23
Coppola, Francis Ford, 22–23, 92–93, 182–83, 188–89
Corman, Roger, 92–93
Courtland, Jerome, 16–17
Cox, Wally, 106–07
Crawford, Christina, 22–23
Crawford, Joan, 14–15, 16–17, 18–19, 20–21, 22–23, 60–61, 76–77, 92–93, 110–11, 148–49, 150–51, 152–53, 156–57, 162–63, 166–67, 174–75, 184–85, 186–87, 188–89, 190–91
Crosby, Bing, 26–27, 46–47, 60–61, 78–79, 162–63
Crumb, R., 202–03
Cruz, Maria, 106–07
Cukor, George, 118–19, 134–35, 184–85
Curtis, Tony, 46–47, 126–27
Curtiz, Michael, 184–85

Daisy, The, 138–39
Dali, Salvador, 124–25
Damone, Vic, 30–31
Darin, Bobby, 4–5
Darvi, Bella, 2–3
David, Hal, 44–45

Davidson, Bill, 122–23
Davies, Marion, 54–55, 58–59, 88–89, 146–47, 158–59, 160–61, 198–99
Davis, Bette, 2–3, 6–7, 14–15, 46–47, 50–51, 58–59, 60–61, 72–73, 76–77, 80–81, 98–99, 100–01, 112–13, 152–53, 162–63, 168–69, 186–87, 190–91, 194–95
Davis, Glenn, 130–31
Davis, Sammy, Jr., 86–87, 100–01
Davis, Ossie, 54–55
Day, Doris, 82–83, 100–01, 182–83
DeAbrasso, Countess Dorothy, 58–59
De Havilland, Olivia, 4–5, 24–25, 30–31, 162–63
Dean, James, 10–11, 30–31, 74–75, 92–93, 138–39
Del Rio, Dolores, 58–59
DeMille, Cecil B., 70–71, 74–75, 144–45, 150–51, 154–55, 160–61, 164–65, 196–97
DeNiro, Robert, 52–53
DePalma, Brian, 64–65
Derek, Bo, 182–83
DeRita, Joe, 24–25
Devoe, Daisy, 58–59
Dexter, Anthony, 82–83
Diamond, I. A. L., 172–73
Dietrich, Marlene, 30–31, 46–47, 98–99, 128–29
Dillinger, John, 50–51
Dillion, Josephine, 116–17
DiMaggio, Joe, 126–27
Directors Guild, 42–43
Disney, Walt, 10–11, 16–17, 18–19, 26–27, 40–41, 42–43, 44–45, 54–55, 72–73, 114–15, 154–55, 158–59, 166–67, 186–87
Dmytryk, Edward, 42–43
Domino, Fats, 12–13
Donald Duck, 48–49
Donlevy, Brian, 110–11
Douglas, Kirk, 24–25, 72–73, 78–79, 162–63, 174–75, 186–87
Douglas, Michael, 6–7, 72–73, 94–95
Douglas, Nathan E., 42–43
Drake, Betsy, 120–21
Dreiser, Theodore, 94–95
Dumont, Margaret, 78–79
Dunaway, Faye, 92–93
Dunne, Irene, 58–59
Dunne, Phillip, 42–43
Du Pont, Mariana, 120–21
Durbin, Deanna, 20–21
Dwan, Alan, 174–75

Eagels, Jeanne, 38–39
Eastwood, Clint, 6–7, 16–17, 18–19, 62–63
Ebert, Roger, 100–01
Ebsen, Buddy, 134–35
Eddy, Nelson, 160–61
Edington, Frank, 178–79
Edison, Thomas Alva, 36–37
Edwards, Blake, 140–41
Egan, Richard, 174–75
Egyptian Theater, 146–47
Eisenstein, Sergei, 148–49
Eldridge, Florence, 78–79
Ellington, Duke, 144–45
Entwistle, Peg, 144–45
E.T., 100–01
Ewell, Tom, 12–13

Fabian, 62–63
Factor, Max, 192–93
Factory, The, 138–39
Fairbanks, Douglas, 6–7, 24–25, 38–39, 58–59, 110–11, 144–45, 146–47, 158–59, 160–61
Fairbanks, Douglas, Jr., 14–15
Falcon Lair, 150–51
Fane, Frank, 140–41
Farrell, Charles, 104–05
Farrow, Mia, 202–03
Faulkner, William, 6–7, 180–81
Fawcett, Farrah, 30–31, 174–75
Fazenda, Louise, 160–61
Feldman, Charles K., 90–91, 178–79
Fetchit, Stepin, 54–55, 96–97
Fidler, Jimmy, 80–81, 138–39
Field, Sally, 66–67
Fields, W.C., 140–41, 190–91
Finch, Peter, 10–11, 44–45
Fine, Larry, 24–25
Fisher, Eddie, 80–81, 100–01, 130–31, 200–01
Fitzgerald, F. Scott, 58–59, 80–81, 82–83, 138–39, 180–81
Flaherty, Robert, 202–03
Fleming, Victor, 14–15, 118–19, 134–35
Flynn, Errol, 10–11, 30–31, 80–81, 138–39, 142–43, 186–87, 198–99
Fonda, Henry, 22–23, 58–59, 84–85, 128–29
Fonda, Jane, 6–7, 52–53, 60–61, 74–75, 100–01, 142–43
Fonda, Peter, 22–23, 92–93
Ford, Glenn, 2–3, 110–11, 168–69
Ford, John, 48–49, 184–85
Forest Lawn Cemetery, 164–65
Forman, Milos, 62–63
Foster, Preston, 160–61

**207**

Fox. See Twentieth Century Fox.
Francis, Connie, 12–13
Francis, Lee, 198–99
Frank, Anne, 20–21
Frankenstein, 36–37, 84–85
Frederick's of Hollywood, 152–53
Freed, Arthur, 134–35
Freud, Sigmund, 80–81
Funicello, Annette, 16–17
Furthman, Jules, 6–7

Gable, Clark, 2–3, 14–15, 16–17, 44–45, 50–51, 58–59, 66–67, 78–79, 86–87, 98–99, 100–01, 110–11, 116–17, 118–19, 126–27, 150–51, 152–53, 158–59, 178–79, 190–91
Gable, John Clark, 116–17
Gabor, Zsa Zsa, 2–3, 100–01
Garbo, Greta, 46–47, 76–77, 82–83, 100–01, 148–49, 176–77, 178–79, 184–85, 194–95
Garden of Allah, 58–59, 138–39
Gardner, Ava, 74–75, 140–41, 194–95
Garfield, John, 10–11, 24–25, 98–99
Garland, Judy, 22–23, 54–55, 62–63, 84–85, 86–87, 116–17, 134–35, 142–43, 156–57, 162–63, 178–79, 184–85
Garner, James, 156–57
Gehrig, Lou, 88–89
Geisler, Jerry, 186–87
Getty, J. Paul, 74–75
Gibbons, Cedric, 66–67
Gilbert, John, 38–39, 86–87, 150–51
Gleason, Jackie, 168–69
Glyn, Madam Elinor, 38–39
Goddard, Paulette, 118–19
Goldman, Albert, 2–3
Gold's Gym, 142–43
Goldwyn, Samuel, 76–77, 78–79, 84–85, 90–91, 94–95, 162–63, 166–67, 176–77
Gordon, Ruth, 92–93
Gorgeous George, 18–19
Gough, Lloyd, 42–43
Grable, Betty, 62–63
Graham, Sheilah, 14–15, 18–19, 58–59, 80–81, 112–13, 158–59
Granger, Stewart, 80–81
Grant, Cary, 30–31, 46–47, 58–59, 80–81, 82–83, 90–91, 120–21, 124–25, 186–87
Grauman, Sid, 14–15, 146–47
Grauman's Chinese Theater, 60–61, 86–87, 146–47, 152–53
Greenacres, 198–99
Greenstreet, Sydney, 90–91, 168–69
Grey, Lita, 2–3

Griffith, D. W., 36–37, 38–39, 142–43, 144–45, 176–77
Griffith Park Observatory, 92–93, 178–79
Gurie, Sigrid, 76–77
Guy, Ramon, 110–11

Haines, William, 84–85
Haley, Jack, 134–35
Hall, Huntz, 82–83
Hamilton, George, 96–97, 150–51
Hamilton, Margaret, 134–35
Hardy, Andy, 96–97
Hardy, Oliver, 26–27, 28–29
Harlow, Jean, 26–27, 58–59, 90–91, 128–29, 164–65, 180–81, 202–03
Harrison, Rex, 82–83
Harrison, Robert, 80–81
Hart, William S., 38–39, 194–95
Haver, June, 154–55
Hawks, Howard, 26–27, 28–29, 50–51, 82–83, 88–89, 100–01, 180–81, 184–85
Hayakawa, Sessue, 154–55
Hayes, Helen, 54–55, 118–19
Hayes, John Michael, 172–73
Hays, Wayne L., 116–17
Hays, Will H., 56–57
Hayward, Leland, 162–63
Hayward, Susan, 62–63
Hayworth, Rita, 2–3, 16–17, 50–51, 168–69
Head, Edith, 140–41, 160–61, 194–95
Hearst, William Randolph, 8–9, 56–57, 58–59, 86–87, 88–89, 146–47, 158–59, 172–73, 198–99
Hecht, Ben, 94–95, 190–91
Hedren, Tippi, 70–71, 124–25
Hellman, Lillian, 56–57, 90–91, 130–31
Hemingway, Ernest, 6–7, 66–67, 180–81
Henreid, Paul, 112–13
Henry, Buck, 172–73
Hepburn, Katharine, 6–7, 24–25, 46–47, 72–73, 96–97, 118–19, 122–23, 162–63, 166–67, 190–91, 192–93, 198–99
Hepburn, Dr. Thomas Norval, 122–23
Heston, Charlton, 22–23
Higham, Charles, 76–77
Hillcrest Country Club, 144–45, 176–77
Hilton, Nicky, 160–61, 200–01
Hinckley, John W., Jr., 52–53
Hitchcock, Alfred, 22–23, 32–33, 48–49, 98–99, 124–25, 128–29, 172–73, 174–75, 176–77, 180–81
Hoffman, Dustin, 32–33, 46–47, 168–69, 188–89
Holden, William, 164–65
Holliday, Judy, 78–79, 184–85

Hollywood Boulevard, 98–99, 138–39, 146–47, 148–49
Hollywood Canteen, 98–99
Hollywood Conservatory of Music, 156–57
Hollywood High School, 156–57
Hollywood Hotel, 138–39
Hollywood Memorial Cemetery, 164–65
Hollywood Memorial Park, 160–61
Hollywood Professional School, 156–57
Hollywood Roosevelt Hotel, 148–49
Hollywood Ten, 42–43
Hollywood Theater, 146–47
Holmby Hills Rat Pack, 84–85
Hooper, Tobe, 92–93
Hoover, J. Edgar, 26–27
Hope, Bob, 26–27, 60–61
Hopper, Hedda, 32–33, 80–81, 128–29, 140–41, 162–63, 188–89
Horne, Lena, 54–55, 82–83
Hotel Dunbar, 144–45
House Committee on Un-American Activities (HUAC), 42–43
House of Francis, 198–99
Hovey, Walter, 36–37
Howard, Curly, 24–25
Howard, Leslie, 50–51, 58–59, 104–05, 166–67
Howard, Moe, 24–25
Howard, Shemp, 24–25
Hudson, Rock, 174–75
Hughes, Howard, 24–25, 72–73, 76–77, 94–95, 140–41, 160–61, 190–91, 200–01
Hulce, Tom, 62–63
Hunt, Linda, 46–47
Hunt, Terry, 98–99
Hunter, Ross, 182–83
Huston, John, 32–33, 42–43, 48–49, 180–81, 184–85
Huston, Walter, 32–33
Hutton, Barbara, 2–3
Hutton, Timothy, 62–63
Hyams, Joe, 80–81
Hyde, John, 178–79

I. Magnin, 152–53
Ince, Thomas, 86–87
International Creative Management (ICM), 28–29, 178–79

Jackson, Anne, 32–33
Jackson, Michael, 142–43
Jaffe, Sam, 104–05
Jarman, Claude, Jr., 20–21
Jessel, George, 72–73
Johansson, Ingemar, 130–31

John, Elton, 150–51
Johnson, Jack, 24–25, 96–97
Johnson, Lynda Bird, 96–97
Johnston, Eric, 42–43
Jolson, Al, 54–55, 72–73, 178–79
Joseph, Jackie, 158–59

Kalem Company, 186–87
Kalmus, Dr. Herbert Thomas, 196–97
Kanter, Hal, 172–73
Karloff, Boris, 36–37, 64–65, 84–85, 192–93
Karno Company, 38–39
Kasdan, Lawrence, 172–73
Kashfi, Anna, 106–07
Kaufmann, George S., 30–31, 138–39
Kaye, Danny, 78–79, 144–45
Kazan, Elia, 56–57
Keaton, Buster, 28–29, 140–41, 150–51
Keeler, Ruby, 166–67
Kellerman, Sally, 156–57
Kelley, Kitty, 130–31
Kelly, Gene, 26–27, 62–63, 140–41, 168–69
Kelly, Grace, 80–81, 126–27
Kelly, John Orry, 186–87, 194–95
Kennedy, Jacqueline, 52–53
Kennedy, John F., 2–3, 52–53, 126–27
Kennedy, Joseph P., 108–09, 158–59
Kerr, Deborah, 82–83
Kevan, Jack, 192–93
Keystone Kops, 8–9, 58–59
Keystone Studio, 36–37
Khan, Prince Ali, 84–85
Kilgallen, Dorothy, 188–89
King Kong, 142–43
Kosleck, Martin, 24–25
Kramer, Stanley, 182–83

Ladd, Alan, 20–21, 78–79, 82–83, 196–97
Ladd, Alan, Jr., 72–73
Ladd, Cheryl, 20–21
Ladd, David, 20–21
LADIES, 158–59
Laemmle, Carl, 144–45
Lahr, Bert, 134–35
Lake, Veronica, 60–61
Lamarr, Hedy, 90–91, 152–53
Lancaster, Burt, 52–53, 160–61
Lang, Jennings, 182–83
Langdon, Harry, 108–09
Lange, Jessica, 44–45
Langhan, Ria, 116–17
Lardner, Ring, Jr., 42–43
Lasky, Jesse L., 24–25
Lassie, 20–21

Laughton, Charles, 64–65
Laurel, Stan, 26–27, 28–29
Lauren, Ralph, 194–95
Lavender Lady, The, 168–69
Lawford, Peter, 126–27, 150–51
Lawson, John Howard, 42–43
Lee, Bruce, 26–27
Leigh, Vivien, 2–3, 14–15, 24–25, 76–77, 164–65
Lemmon, Jack, 46–47, 184–85
Leonard, Jack E., 96–97
Lerner, Max, 130–31
Levant, Oscar, 100–01
Levine, Joseph E., 182–83
Lewis, Jerry, 26–27, 44–45, 158–59
Lewis, Jerry Lee, 12–13
Lewis, Patti, 158–59
Lewis, Sinclair, 54–55
Liberace, 80–81, 88–89
Liston, Sonny, 96–97
Litvak, Anatole, 48–49
Lloyd, Harold, 30–31, 144–45, 198–99
Logan, Joshua, 126–27, 188–89
Lombard, Carole, 58–59, 116–17, 124–25, 150–51, 158–59, 174–75, 188–89, 200–01
Loos, Anita, 36–37
Lord, Father, 74–75
Loren, Sophia, 120–21, 162–63
Lorre, Peter, 64–65, 98–99
Los Angeles Country Club, 160–61
Loy, Myrna, 14–15, 50–51, 156–57
Lucas, George, 28–29, 72–73, 156–57, 182–83
Lugosi, Bela, 10–11, 94–95
Luke, Keye, 192–93
Lytess, Natasha, 126–27

MacArthur, Gen. Douglas, 154–55
MacDonald, Jeanette, 16–17
MacLaine, Shirley, 40–41, 174–75
MacMurray, Fred, 44–45, 154–55, 180–81
Madden, Owney, 50–51
Maltz, Albert, 42–43
Ma Maison, 198–99
Mankiewicz, Herman, 100–01, 172–73
Mann, Thomas, 148–49
Mansfield, Jayne, 12–13, 86–87, 150–51
Mantee, Duke, 50–51
March, Frederic, 40–41
Martin, Dean, 26–27, 44–45, 88–89
Martin, Dr. Harry "Docky", 158–59
Marvin, Lee, 62–63, 186–87
Marx, Groucho, 60–61, 100–01, 144–45, 162–63
Marx, Harpo, 78–79

Marx Brothers, 22–23, 60–61, 176–77
Mason, James, 142–43, 150–51
Massey, Raymond, 64–65, 104–05
Matthau, Walter, 184–85
Mature, Victor, 16–17, 162–63
Maugham, Somerset, 16–17, 126–27
Max Factor Beauty Museum, 144–45
May Company, 152–53
Mayer, Louis B., 20–21, 84–85, 86–87, 134–35, 150–51, 160–61, 162–63, 176–77, 178–79, 190–91, 192–93
McCarthy, Charlie, 54–55
McCarthy, Eugene, 96–97
McCarthy, Joseph, 132–33
McCarthy, Kevin, 32–33
McCrea, Joel, 156–57
McDaniel, Hattie, 54–55
McKinley, William, 52–53
McLaglen, Victor, 24–25, 168–69
Meade, Bill, 10–11
Mengers, Sue, 140–41, 178–79
Menjou, Adolphe, 6–7, 90–91
Merrill, Gary, 2–3
Methot, Mayo, 104–05
Metro-Goldwyn-Mayer, 20–21, 22–23, 54–55, 66–67, 74–75, 76–77, 84–85, 88–89, 128–29, 130–31, 134–35, 158–59, 160–61, 176–77, 178–79, 180–81, 182–83, 198–99
Metro-Goldwyn-Mayer-United Artists, 88–89
Michener, James, 74–75
Mickey Mouse, 24–25, 114–15, 142–43
Miles, Sarah, 86–87
Miller, Arthur, 126–27
Mills, Hayley, 114–15
Mineo, Sal, 10–11, 50–51, 74–75, 96–97
Minnelli, Liza, 22–23
Minnelli, Vincente, 22–23
Minter, Mary Miles, 10–11
Mirisch, David, 174–75
Mitchell, Margaret, 118–19
Mitchum, Robert, 186–87
Mix, Tom, 38–39, 148–49, 150–51
Mobley, Mary Ann, 12–13
Mocambo Club, 54–55
Monroe, Marilyn, 6–7, 32–33, 110–11, 116–17, 126–27, 140–41, 164–65, 178–79, 190–91
Montand, Yves, 126–27
Montgomery, Robert, 44–45
Monti, Carlotta, 140–41
Montmartre Cafe, 148–49
Moon, Reverend Sun Myung, 154–55
Moore, Terry, 24–25, 72–73, 172–73
Moreno, Rita, 106–07

Morris, Philip, 76–77
Mostel, Zero, 42–43
Motion Picture Association of America, 42–43
Motion Picture Country House, The, 144–45
Motion Picture Producers Association, 108–09
Mount Lee, 144–54
Mr. Blackwell, 46–47
Mr. T, 18–19
Mulholland, William, 94–95
Mulray, Hollis, 94–95
Muni, Paul, 50–51, 54–55, 190–91
Muse, Clarence, 54–55
Musso and Frank Grill, 148–49
Myrick, Susan, 118–19

National Legion of Decency, 154–55
Nazimova, Alla, 138–39
Negri, Pola, 16–17, 28–29
Nelson, Ricky, 88–89
Newman, Paul, 30–31, 96–97, 152–53, 166–67
Nicholson, James, 182–83
Nilsson, Anna Q., 140–41
Niven, David, 40–41, 58–59, 84–85, 188–89
Nixon, Pat, 88–89
Nixon, Richard M., 52–53, 94–95
Noguchi, Thomas T., 164–65
Normand, Mabel, 8–9, 10–11
Novak, Kim, 86–87, 168–69
Nureyev, Rudolph, 82–83

Oberon, Merle, 58–59, 140–41
O'Brien, Margaret, 20–21
Ocean House, 198–99
O'Connor, Donald, 150–51
Odlum, Floyd, 200–01
O'Doul, Lefty, 4–5
Oland, Warner, 4–5
Olivier, Laurence, 40–41, 84–85
O'Neal, Ryan, 22–23, 156–57, 174–75
O'Neal, Tatum, 22–23
O'Neill, Jennifer, 74–75
Opel, Robert, 40–41
Oppenheimer, George, 76–77
Orbison, Roy, 78–79
Ornitz, Sam, 42–43
Orry Kelly, John. See Kelly, John Orry.
Orsatti, Frank, 178–79
Oscar. See Academy Awards.
O'Sullivan, Maureen, 56–57
Our Gang, 20–21

Paar, Jack, 112–13
Paley, William, 110–11
Pantages Theater, 146–47
Paramount Studios, 38–39, 60–61, 88–89, 124–25, 194–95
Parker, Dorothy, 90–91, 122–23, 138–39, 180–81
Parker, Fess, 114–15
Parsons, Louella, 80–81, 138–39, 158–59
Pathé Pictures, 148–49, 158–59
Pawley, Bill, 130–31
Peck, Gregory, 82–83
Peckinpah, Sam, 100–01
Perkins, Anthony, 66–67
Pickford, Mary, 6–7, 14–15, 36–37, 38–39, 58–59, 82–83, 110–11, 146–47, 152–53, 158–59, 176–77
Pierce, Jack, 192–93
Pitts, Zasu, 38–39, 54–55
Platters, The, 12–13
Plunkett, Walter, 194–95
Poitier, Sidney, 54–55, 158–59
Polanski, Roman, 184–85
Pollack, Sydney, 184–85
Polo Lounge, 142–43, 148–49
Ponti, Carlo, 120–21
Posh Bagel, The, 8–9
Power, Tyrone, 58–59, 88–89, 192–93, 198–99
Preminger, Otto, 52–53, 82–83
Presley, Elvis, 2–3, 12–13, 16–17, 78–79, 82–83, 172–73
Price, Vincent, 64–65, 166–67
Pryor, Richard, 172–73
Puzo, Mario, 44–45

Quinn, Anthony, 64–65, 66–67, 74–75

Raft, George, 10–11, 50–51, 82–83
Rainier, Prince, 126–27
Rains, Claude, 84–85, 200–01
Rambova, Natasha, 150–51
Randolph, John, 42–43
Rapf, Harry, 174–75, 182–83
Rappe, Virginia, 58–59
Rathbone, Basil, 58–59
Reagan, Ronald, 2–3, 42–43, 52–53, 128–29
Redford, Robert, 30–31, 184–85, 194–95
Redgrave, Vanessa, 8–9
Reid, Dorothy, 164–65
Reid, Wallace, 164–65
Republic Pictures, 132–33
Rex, The, 186–87
Reynolds, Burt, 8–9, 52–53, 62–63, 66–67, 76–77, 86–87, 96–97, 150–51, 200–01

**211**

Reynolds, Debbie, 4–5, 62–63
Rich, Robert, 42–43
Rin Tin Tin, 140–41, 176–77
Riskin, Robert, 66–67, 116–17
Ritt, Martin, 42–43
Rivera, Diego, 192–93
RKO Pictures, 62–63, 160–61, 200–01
Robards, Jason, 156–57
Robb, Charles, 96–97
Robertson, Cliff, 12–13
Robinson, Edward G., 50–51, 104–05, 178–79
Rodeo Drive, 138–39, 148–49
Rogers, Ginger, 22–23, 24–25, 30–31, 62–63, 78–79, 90–91, 98–99, 128–29, 160–61, 162–63
Rogers, Lela, 22–23, 42–43
Rogers, Roy, 4–5
Rogers, Will, 6–7, 90–91, 166–67, 168–69
Romanoff's, 104–05, 138–39, 148–49
Romero, Cesar, 98–99
Romero, George, 64–65
Rooney, Mickey, 6–7, 54–55, 96–97, 156–57
Roosevelt, Eleanor, 52–53
Roosevelt, Franklin D., 52–53
Roosevelt, Theodore, 52–53
Rose, Helen, 194–95
Ross, Katharine, 30–31
Rowland, Richard, 176–77
Rubirosa, Porfirio, 2–3
Russell, Harold, 48–49
Russell, Jane, 26–27, 76–77, 200–01
Russell, Rosalind, 30–31, 82–83
Ruth, Babe, 88–89
Rutherford, Ann, 96–97

Sands, Tommy, 62–63
San Simeon, 8–9, 58–59, 146–47
Schiaparelli, 152–53
Schockley, William, 156–57
Schrader, Paul, 154–55
Schwab's Drugstore, 76–77, 80–81, 144–45
Schwarzenegger, Arnold, 142–43
Scorsese, Martin, 92–93, 184–85
Scott, Adrian, 42–43
Scott, George C., 168–69
Scott, Randolph, 58–59, 120–21, 160–61, 166–67
Screen Actors Guild, 42–43
Screen Directors Guild, 108–09
Screen Writers Guild, 42–43
Sebastian, Ray, 192–93
Sedgwick, Edward, 160–61
Segal, George, 158–59, 168–69
Segal, Marion, 158–59

Selig, Col. William, 52–53
Sellers, Peter, 188–89
Selznick, David O., 76–77, 118–19, 124–25, 140–41, 176–77, 200–01
Selznick, Myron, 178–79
Sennett, Mack, 8–9, 36–37, 58–59, 190–91, 202–03
Shearer, Norma, 58–59
Shelley, Joshua, 42–43
Shelley, Mary Wollstonecraft, 92–93
Shepard, Sam, 180–81
Sheridan, Ann, 46–47
Shields, Brooke, 20–21
Shields, Jimmy, 84–85
Short, Elizabeth, 164–65
Shrine Auditorium, 142–43
Siegel, Bugsy, 98–99, 176–77
Simmons, Jean, 160–61
Simms, Larry, 20–21
Simon, Carly, 94–95
Simon, Neil, 88–89, 172–73
Sinatra, Frank, 84–85, 126–27, 140–41
Siskel, Gene, 100–01
Skolsky, Sidney, 80–81
Skouras, Spyros, 202–03
Smith, Bessie, 54–55
Smith, Kate, 88–89
Smith, Ludlow Ogden, 122–23
SPCA Pet Memorial Park, 146–47
Spellman, Cardinal, 56–57
Spielberg, Steven, 18–19, 40–41, 94–95, 172–73, 184–85, 188–89
Spillane, Mickey, 28–29
Spitz, Carl, 134–35
Spitz, Mark, 40–41
Spoor, George, 26–27
Stanford, Sally, 28–29
Stanwyck, Barbara, 174–75
Steele, Alfred, 110–11
Stengel, Casey, 164–65
Stern, Isaac, 24–25
Stewart, Jimmy, 30–31, 124–25, 128–29, 178–79
Stills, Alfred, 162–63
Strasberg, Lee, 126–27
Strasburg, Paula, 126–27
Stravinsky, Igor, 148–49
Streisand, Barbra, 82–83, 178–79
Studio One, 138–39
Sullavan, Margaret, 162–63
Sullivan, Ed, 6–7, 14–15, 126–27
Sunset Strip, 146–47
Svengali Productions, 182–83
Swanson, Gloria, 16–17, 38–39, 82–83, 160–61

Talmadge, Norma, 198–99
Taylor, Elizabeth, 4–5, 14–15, 20–21, 28–29, 66–67, 74–75, 80–81, 100–01, 130–31, 142–43, 152–53, 160–61, 164–65, 190–91, 194–95, 198–99, 202–03
Taylor, James, 94–95
Taylor, Samuel, 158–59
Taylor, William Desmond, 10–11
Technicolor, 196–97, 202–03
Temple, Shirley, 2–3, 16–17, 54–55, 78–79, 94–95, 190–91
Teriipaia, Tarita, 106–07
Thalberg, Irving, 176–77, 182–83
Thomas, Bob, 110–11
Thorpe, Richard, 134–35
Three Stooges, The, 24–25, 32–33
Todd, Mike, 10–11, 96–97, 164–65, 182–83, 200–01
Tone, Franchot, 110–11
Toomey, Regis, 200–01
Torrence, Ernest, 160–61
Towne, Robert, 92–93, 172–73
Tracy, Spencer, 14–15, 26–27, 44–45, 72–73, 110–11, 122–23, 154–55, 166–67, 192–93
Tramont, Jean-Claude, 178–79
Triangle Film Company, 38–39
Trocadero, 98–99
Trotsky, Leon, 88–89
Trumbo, Dalton, 42–43, 162–63
Truscott, John, 8–9
Tryon, Tom, 154–55
Tufts, Sonny, 92–93
Turner, Lana, 44–45, 76–77, 118–19, 128–29, 156–57, 182–83
Turner, Ted, 88–89
Twentieth Century-Fox, 72–73, 104–05, 130–31, 142–43, 154–55, 174–75, 176–77, 202–03
Tyson, Cicely, 74–75

Ullman, Liv, 44–45
Unification Church, 154–55
United Artists, 176–77
Universal Studios, 18–19, 20–21, 64–65, 144–45, 146–47

Valens, Richie, 12–13
Valentino, Rudolph, 28–29, 38–39, 82–83, 138–139, 150–51, 160–61, 194–95
Van Cleve, Edith, 106–07
Veidt, Conrad, 82–83
Velez, Lupe, 96–97
Venice Pier, 58–59
Vidal, Gore, 100–01
Vidor, King, 28–29, 134–35

Villa Capri, 138–39
Von Sternberg, Josef, 94–95
Von Stroheim, Erich, 36–37, 38–39, 176–77

Wagner, Robert, 66–67
Wallace, Lew, 186–87
Wallach, Eli, 32–33
Wallis, Hal, 52–53, 174–75, 178–79
Wallis, Minna, 178–79
Walsh, Raoul, 174–75
Walt Disney Studios, 94–95, 142–43. *See also* Disney, Walt.
Wanger, Walter, 182–83
Wansell, Geoffrey, 120–21
Warner, H. B., 140–41
Warner, Jack, 42–43, 100–01, 166–67, 176–77
Warner, John, 200–01
Warner Brothers Studios, 72–73, 104–05, 158–59, 176–77, 184–85, 194–95
Warren, Earl, 186–87
Washington, Dinah, 144–45
Washington, Mildred, 54–55
Wasserman, Lew, 178–79
Wayne, John, 6–7, 14–15, 88–89, 132–33, 156–57, 174–75, 188–89
Weaver, Dennis, 184–85
Weissmuller, Johnny, 56–57
Welch, Raquel, 30–31
Weld, Tuesday, 12–13
Welles, Orson, 52–53, 56–57, 90–91, 100–01, 172–73
Wellman, William, Jr., 12–13
West, Mae, 90–91, 120–21, 142–43, 146–47, 152–53, 158–59, 190–91, 198–99
West, Nathanael, 180–81
Westmore, Bud, 192–93
Westmore, George, 78–79
Westmore, Percy, 192–93
White, Loray, 86–87
Whiting, David A., 86–87
Whitney, Iris, 10–11
Widmark, Richard, 84–85
Wilcox, Horace, 154–55
Wilder, Billy, 184–85
Wilder, Thornton, 180–81
Wilding, Michael, 80–81, 130–31, 200–01
Wilkerson, Billy, 76–77, 98–99, 158–59
William Morris Agency, 40–41, 178–79
Williams, Andy, 62–63
Williams, Cindy, 18–19
Williams, Tennessee, 56–57
Wills, Chill, 18–19
Willson, Harry, 174–75
Wilson, Bob, 28–29
Wilson, Dooley, 82–83

**213**

Wilson, Woodrow, 52–53
Winchell, Walter, 80–81, 86–87, 112–13
Winters, Jonathan, 112–13
Winters, Shelley, 78–79
Wolfe, Thomas, 180–81
Wood, Natalie, 10–11, 56–57, 66–67, 74–75, 156–57, 164–65
Wood, Sam, 118–19
Woodward, Joanne, 160–61
Woolley, Monty, 52–53
Wray, Fay, 56–57
Wright, Frank Lloyd, 22–23
Wyler, William, 36–37, 42–43, 46–49
Wyman, Jane, 2–3, 200–01

Young, Loretta, 66–67, 86–87, 118–19, 154–55
Young, Ned, 42–43

Zanuck, Darryl F., 2–3, 48–49, 78–79, 166–67, 176–77, 192–93

# INDEX TO MOVIES

Absent-Minded Professor, The (1961), 44–45
Action in the North Atlantic (1943), 104–05
Adventures of Marco Polo, The (1938), 76–77
Adventures of Robin Hood, The (1938), 4–5
African Queen, The (1951), 10–11, 180–81
Agony and the Ecstasy, The (1965), 154–55
Airport (1969), 182–83
Alamo, The (1960), 188–89
Algiers (1938), 90–91
Alice Doesn't Live Here Anymore (1975), 168–69, 184–85
All About Eve (1950), 22–23, 202–03
All Night Long (1981), 178–79
All Quiet on the Western Front (1930), 48–49
Amadeus (1984), 62–63
American Graffiti (1973), 72–73, 156–57
American Tragedy, An (1931), 94–95
Anatomy of a Murder (1959), 128–29
Anchors Away (1945), 26–27
Angels with Dirty Faces (1938), 50–51
Anna Christie (1930), 176–77
Annie (1982), 188–89
Annie Hall (1977), 32–33
Anthony Adverse (1936), 200–01
Apartment, The (1960), 172–73
Around The World in Eighty Days (1956), 182–83, 200–01
Arrowsmith (1931), 54–55

Arsenic and Old Lace (1944), 64–65, 120–21
Attack of the Crab Monsters (1957), 92–93
Attack of the Killer Tomatoes (1978), 92–93

Baby Doll (1956), 56–57
Back to Bataan (1944), 84–85
Bad and the Beautiful, The (1952), 140–41
Barkleys of Broadway, The (1949), 162–63
Battle of Midway, The (1942), 48–49
Battle of San Pietro, The (1944), 48–49
Beach Blanket Bingo (1965), 182–83
Beast With Five Fingers, The (1946), 64–65
Beau Geste (1939), 4–5
Becky Sharp (1934), 88–89, 202–03
Beloved Infidel (1959), 82–83
Ben Hur (1907), 186–87
Ben Hur (1959), 36–37, 42–43
Bend of the River (1952), 178–79
Best Years of Our Lives, The (1946), 36–37, 48–49
Beyond the Forest (1949), 112–13
Big Broadcast of 1938 (1938), 60–61
Big Business (1929), 28–29
Big Sleep, The (1946), 28–29, 184–85
Big Trail, The (1929), 132–33
Bill of Divorcement, A (1932), 122–23
Birds, The (1963), 70–71, 124–25
Birth of a Nation, The (1915), 36–37, 52–53, 56–57, 142–43
Black Pirate, The (1926), 38–39
Blazing Saddles (1974), 24–25, 172–73
Blue Bird, The (1976), 74–75
Blue Dahlia, The (1946), 82–83
Body Double (1984), 184–85
Bonnie and Clyde (1967), 70–71
Born Yesterday (1950), 84–85, 184–85
Boys' Town (1938), 44–45
Brave One, The (1957), 42–43
Bride of Frankenstein (1935), 92–93
Bridge on the River Kwai, The (1957), 72–73, 154–55
Bringing Up Baby (1938), 122–23
Buddy Holly Story, The (1978), 142–43
Bus Stop (1956), 126–27
Butch Cassidy and the Sundance Kid (1969), 30–31

Cain and Mabel (1936), 32–33
California Suite (1978), 142–43
Camelot (1967), 8–9
Camille (1936), 184–85
Captain Newman, M.D. (1963), 4–5
Captains Courageous (1937), 72–73
Caravans (1978), 74–75
Cardinal, The (1963), 154–55

Carefree (1938), 62–63
Carpetbaggers, The (1963), 140–41, 182–83
Carrie (1976), 64–65
Casablanca (1942), 10–11, 18–19, 82–83, 104–05, 184–85, 200–01
Casino Royale (1967), 188–89
Cat Ballou (1965), 24–25
Cat Women on the Moon (1954), 92–93
Catch-22 (1970), 172–73
Champ, The (1932), 40–41
Change of Habit (1969), 12–13
Chapman Report, The (1962), 6–7
Charge of the Light Brigade, The (1936), 30–31
Children's Hour, The (1962), 56–57
China Syndrome, The (1979), 94–95
Chinatown (1974), 94–95, 142–43, 172–73
Circus, The (1928), 40–41
Citizen Kane (1941), 56–57, 172–73
Cleopatra (1963), 130–31, 142–43, 182–83
Close Encounters of the Third Kind (1977), 70–71
Coconuts, The (1929), 60–61
Color Purple, The (1985), 40–41
Confessions of a Nazi Spy (1939), 24–25, 48–49, 176–77
Conqueror, The (1956), 74–75
Conquest (1937), 148–49
Continental Divide (1981), 172–73
Cotton Comes to Harlem (1970), 54–55
Countess from Hong Kong, A (1967), 162–63

Daddy Long Legs (1955), 62–63
Dangerous (1935), 14–15
Darby O'Gill and the Little People (1959), 114–15
Dark Victory (1939), 80–81
Davy Crockett and the River Pirates (1956), 18–19
Davy Crockett, King of the Wild Frontier (1955), 18–19, 114–15
Dawn of the Dead (1979), 64–65
Day of the Dead (1985), 8–9
Day of the Locust, The (1975), 180–81
Dead End (1937), 10–11
Death Wish, 50–51
Defiant Ones, The (1957), 42–43
Deliverance (1972), 96–97
Der Fuehrer's Face (1942), 48–49
Destry Rides Again (1939), 30–31
Diary of a Sergeant (1946), 48–49
Dirty Harry (1971), 16–17
Doctor Doolittle (1968), 74–75
Dolly Sisters, The (1945), 62–63
Double Indemnity (1944), 180–81, 184–85

Dr. Jekyll and Mr. Hyde (1932), 40–41, 72–73
Dr. Jekyll and Mr. Hyde (1941), 192–93
Dr. No (1962), 114–15
Dracula (1931), 64–65, 166–67
Dragon Seed (1944), 192–93
Dressed to Kill (1980), 64–65
Duel (1971), 184–85

Easter Parade (1948), 62–63
East of Eden (1954), 30–31
East Side of Heaven (1939), 46–47
Easy Rider (1969), 92–93
Egyptian, The (1954), 2–3
8½ (1963), 182–83
Empire Strikes Back, The (1980), 28–29, 44–45, 172–73
Enforcer, The (1976), 16–17
Escape from the Planet of the Apes (1971), 96–97
E.T. (1982), 94–95
Every Day's a Holiday (1937), 152–53
Exorcist, The (1973), 70–71
Exorcist II: The Heretic (1977), 44–45

Face Behind the Mask, The (1941), 64–65
Fantasia (1940), 10–11
Farewell to Arms, A (1932), 66–67
Father of the Bride (1950), 160–61
Filmmaker (1968), 182–83
First Blood (1982), 44–45
First Nudie Musical, The (1976), 18–19
Flying Leathernecks (1951), 84–85
Fog, The (1980), 64–65
Follow the Boys (1963), 12–13
For a Few Dollars More (1967), 44–45
Foreign Correspondent (1940), 48–49
Fort Apache (1948), 48–49
Fortune Cookie, The (1966), 172–73
42nd Street (1933), 166–67
Four Horsemen of the Apocalypse, The (1921), 38–39
Frankenstein (1931), 36–37, 64–65, 84–85
Freaks (1932), 64–65
Friendly Persuasion (1956), 62–63
Fritz the Cat (1972), 202–03
Front, The (1976), 42–43
Front Page, The (1931), 82–83
Fultah Fisher's Boarding House (1924), 108–09
Funny Girl (1968), 42–43

Game of Death (1979), 26–27
Gaslight (1944), 184–85
Gauntlet, The (1977), 16–17
Gay Divorcee, The (1934), 98–99

Gentlemen Prefer Blondes (1953), 6–7, 184–85
Georgy Girl (1966), 202–03
Get Yourself a College Girl (1964), 12–13
Ghost of Frankenstein (1942), 84–85
G.I. Blues (1960), 12–13
Gidget (1959), 12–13
Gilda (1946), 2–3
Girl Can't Help It, The (1956), 12–13
Girl Hunters, The (1963), 28–29
G-Men (1935), 50–51
Goddess, The (1958), 140–41
Godfather, The (1972), 44–45, 66–67, 70–71, 106–07
Godfather, Part II (1975), 22–23, 66–67
Go, Johnny, Go (1958), 12–13
Goldie (1931), 202–03
Gone With the Wind (1939), 14–15, 22–23, 54–55, 58–59, 66–67, 84–85, 116–17, 118–19, 180–81, 184–85, 198–99, 200–01
Graduate, The (1967), 82–83, 172–73
Grease (1978), 156–57
Greatest Story Ever Told, The (1965), 74–75
Guess Who's Coming to Dinner (1967), 182–83
Guys and Dolls (1955), 106–07

Halloween (1978), 64–65
Halls of Montezuma (1950), 84–85
Hamlet (1948), 40–41
Harold and Maude (1971), 92–93
Harvey (1950), 128–29
Hearts in Dixie (1929), 54–55
Heaven Can Wait (1978), 44–45
Heaven's Gate (1981), 74–75
Hello Everybody (1933), 88–89
Hell's Angels (1930), 94–95
Hercules (1959), 182–83
Here Comes Mr. Jordan (1941), 44–45
Her Love Story (1924), 38–39
High Noon (1952), 182–83
High School Confidential (1958), 12–13
High Sierra (1941), 10–11
His Girl Friday (1940), 82–83
His Glorious Night (1929), 86–87
Home of the Brave (1949), 182–83
Hotel Imperial (1927), 16–17, 28–29
Houseboat (1958), 121–22
House on Haunted Hill, The (1959), 64–65
Human Wreckage (1923), 164–65
Humoresque (1946), 24–25
Hunchback of Notre Dame, The (1923, 1939, 1957), 64–65, 192–93
Hush, Hush, Sweet Charlotte (1965), 162–63

I Am a Fugitive from a Chain Gang (1932), 50–51
Imitation of Life (1959), 182–83
Inchon (1982), 154–55
Incredible Journey, The (1963), 114–15
Indiana Jones and the Temple of Doom (1984), 44–45
Informer, The (1935), 24–25, 184–85
In Search of the Castaways (1962), 114–15
Intolerance (1916), 144–45
Invasion of the Body Snatchers (1956), 32–33
Invasion of the Body Snatchers (1978), 32–33
Invisible Man, The (1933), 84–85
Irma la Douce (1963), 172–73
Iron Mask, The (1929), 38–39
Island, The (1978), 178–79
It Happened One Night (1934), 48–49, 66–67, 108–09, 116–17, 152–53
It's a Mad Mad Mad Mad World (1963), 32–33
It's a Wonderful Life (1946), 128–29
I Was a Female War Bride (1949), 46–47
I Was a Teenage Werewolf (1957), 182–83

Jason and the Argonauts (1963), 70–71
Jaws (1975), 70–71, 202–03
Jazz Singer, The (1927), 72–73
Jezebel (1938), 46–47
Juarez (1949), 190–91
Judgment at Nuremburg (1961), 182–83
Julia (1977), 72–73
June Bride (1948), 112–13

Killers, The (1946), 52–53
King Kong (1933), 56–57, 70–71, 118–19
King Kong (1976), 142–43
King of Kings, The (1927), 74 75
Kiss and Tell (1945), 16–17

Lady Vanishes, The (1938), 124–25
Lamb, The (1915), 38–39
Land of the Pharaohs (1955), 74–75 184–85
Last Detail, The (1973), 172–/3
Last of Sheila (1973), 140–41
Last of the Mohicans (1936), 118–19
Last Tycoon, The (1976), 82–83
Letter, The (1940), 46–47
Letty Lynton (1932), 152–53
Liberation of L. B. Jones (1970), 36–37
Lifeboat (1943), 32–33, 124–25
Lights of New York, The (1928), 76–77
Lilies of the Fields (1963), 54–55
Little Annie Rooney (1925), 38–39
Little Caesar (1931), 50–51
Little Foxes, The (1941), 46–47, 186–87
Little Lord Fauntleroy (1936), 118–19

Little Shop of Horrors, The (1960), 92–93
Lodger, The (1927), 124–25
Longest Day, The (1962), 48–49, 62–63
Longest Yard, The (1974), 52–53, 200–01
Long Ships, The (1964), 158–59
Looking for Love (1964), 12–13
Lost Horizon (1937), 108–09
Lost Horizon (1973), 44–45
Love Happy (1950), 32–33
Love Me Tender (1956), 16–17
Loving You (1957), 172–73
Lucky Dog (1917), 26–27
Lust for Life (1956), 66–67

M (1931), 64–65
Mad Love (1935), 64–65
Magnum Force (1973), 16–17, 44–45
Maltese Falcon, The (1941), 10–11, 30–31, 32–33, 48–49, 184–85
Manhattan Melodrama (1934), 50–51
Man of a Thousand Faces (1957), 192–93
Man Who Came Back, The (1930), 104–05
Man Who Came to Dinner, The (1941), 52 53
Man Who Knew Too Much, The (1934), 98–99
Man Who Knew Too Much, The (1956), 124–25, 128–29, 172–73
Man Who Loved Cat Dancing, The (1973), 86–87
Man, Woman and Sin (1927), 38–39
Marked Woman (1937), 112–13
Marnie (1964), 124–25
Marty (1955), 172–73
Mary of Scotland (1936), 78–79, 184–85
Mary Poppins (1964), 114–15
Mask of Fu Manchu, The (1932), 4–5
Mean Streets (1973), 184–85
Men, The (1950), 98–99, 182–83
Men of Boys' Town (1941), 44–45
Mildred Pierce (1945), 110–11, 184–85
Misfits, The (1961), 116–17, 126–27
Miss Sadie Thompson (1953), 16–17, 50–51
Mogambo (1953), 44–45
Mommie Dearest (1981), 92–93
Monkey Business (1952), 6–7
Moon Pilot (1962), 26–27
Moon-Spinners, The (1964), 114–15
Mourning Becomes Electra (1947), 82–83
Move Over, Darling (1963), 172–73
Mr. and Mrs. Smith (1941), 124–25
Mr. Deeds Goes to Town (1936), 108–09
Mr. Roberts (1955), 84–85
Mrs. Miniver (1942), 28–29
Mr. Smith Goes to Washington (1939), 48–49, 108–09, 128–29, 200–01

Mummy's Ghost, The (1944), 84–85
Mummy's Tomb, The (1942), 84–85
Murder by Death (1976), 88–89
Mutiny on the Bounty (1962), 106–07
My Fair Lady (1964), 82–83, 194–95
My Little Chickadee (1940), 190–91
My Official Wife (1916), 88–89
Myra Breckinridge (1970), 30–31
Mysterious Dr. Fu Manchu (1929), 4–5

Nanook of the North (1922), 202–03
National Velvet (1944), 130–31, 160–61
Network (1976), 10–11, 172–73
New York Hat, The (1912), 36–37
New York, New York (1977), 184–85
Night of the Living Dead (1968), 64–65
1941 (1979), 188–89
Norma Rae (1979), 72–73
Notorious (1946), 124–25, 200–01
Now, Voyager (1942), 112–13

Old Acquaintance (1943), 112–13
Old Man and the Sea, The (1958), 180–81
Oliver! (1968), 40–41
Once Upon a Honeymoon (1942), 120–21
One Flew Over the Cuckoo's Nest (1975), 66–67, 72–73
One from the Heart (1982), 188–89
On the Waterfront (1954), 66–67
Oscar, The (1966), 140–41
Our Daily Bread (1934), 28–29
Outlaw, The (1943), 26–27, 200–01

Paint Your Wagon (1969), 62–63
Panama Hattie (1942), 54–55
Paper Moon (1973), 22–23
Parent Trap, The (1961), 114–15
Patton (1970), 94–95
Personal Best (1982), 172–73
Petrified Forest, The (1936), 50–51, 104–05
Phantom of the Opera, The (1925), 192–93
Philadelphia Story, The (1940), 128–29, 198–99
Pillow Talk (1959), 182–83
Pinocchio (1940), 114–15
Place in the Sun, A (1951), 94–95, 130–31
Planet of the Apes (1968), 192–93
Pocketful of Miracles (1961), 172–73
Pollyanna (1920), 38–39
Pollyanna (1960), 114–15
Popeye (1980), 114–15
Postman Always Rings Twice, The (1946), 10–11, 44–45
Postman Always Rings Twice, The (1981), 44–45
Pretty Baby (1978), 20–21

Pride and the Passion, The (1957), 120–21
Pride of the Yankees (1942), 4–5, 88–89
Prizzi's Honor (1985), 48–49, 184–85
Protocol (1984), 172–73
Proud Rebel, The (1956), 20–21
Psycho (1960), 22–23, 66–67, 124–25
Psycho II (1983), 66–67
Public Enemy (1931), 8–9, 50–51, 96–97
Pumping Iron (1977), 142–43

Queen Christina (1933), 148–49
Quo Vadis? (1925), 8–9

Raffles (1929), 162–63
Raging Bull (1980), 154–55
Raiders of the Lost Ark (1981), 172–73
Rain (1932), 16–17
Rain People, The (1969), 182–83
Rambo (1985), 44–45
Razor's Edge, The (1946), 22–23
Rear Window (1954), 124–25, 172–73
Rebecca (1939), 124–25, 176–77
Rebel Without a Cause (1955), 10–11, 74–75, 92–93
Red Dust (1932), 44–45
Red Line 7000 (1965), 184–85
Reluctant Dragon, The (1941), 114–15
Return of Dr. X (1939), 104–05
Return of the Jedi (1983), 172–73
Right Stuff, The (1984), 180–81
Ring of Fear (1954), 28–29
Rio Bravo (1959), 88–89, 184–85
Road to Bali, The (1952), 26–27, 172–73
Road to Utopia, The (1945), 60–61
Roaring Twenties, The (1939), 50–51
Robe, The (1953), 202–03
Robin Hood (1922), 38–39, 144–45
Rock Around the Clock (1956), 12–13
Rock, Rock, Rock (1956), 12–13
Rocky III (1982), 18–19
Rope (1948), 124–25, 130–31
Russians Are Coming, the Russians Are Coming, The (1966), 74–75

Saboteur (1942), 180–81
St. Louis Blues (1928), 54–55
Sands of Iwo Jima (1949), 84–85
San Francisco (1936), 16–17
Saratoga (1937), 26–27
Saskatchewan (1954), 78–79
Scared Stiff (1953), 26–27
Scarface (1932), 50–51, 184–85, 190–91
Sea Wife (1957), 16–17
Sergeant York (1941), 160–61
Seventh Voyage of Sinbad, The (1958), 70–71

Seven Year Itch, The (1955), 6–7, 126–27
Sex Hygiene (1941), 48–49
Shadow of a Doubt (1943), 180–81
Shampoo (1975), 172–73
She Done Him Wrong (1933), 90–91, 121–22, 198–99
Sheik, The (1921), 38–39, 138–39
Silk Stockings (1957), 62–63
Sincerely Yours (1955), 88–89
Singing Sandy (1935), 132–33
Singin' in the Rain (1952), 140–41
Skippy (1931), 86–87
Smokey and the Bandit (1977), 66–67
Snow White and the Seven Dwarfs (1938), 72–73
S.O.B. (1981), 140–41
Solomon and Sheba (1958), 198–99
Some Like It Hot (1959), 6–7, 46–47, 126–27, 172–73, 184–85
Song of the South (1947), 54–55
Son of Dracula (1943), 84–85
Son of Flubber (1963), 44–45
South Pacific (1958), 188–89
Spartacus (1960), 162–63
Spellbound (1945), 124–25
Splash (1984), 142–43
Splendor in the Grass (1961), 56–57
Squaw Man, The (1913), 144–45
Stagecoach (1939), 24–25, 48–49, 132–33
Stage Fright (1950), 22–23
Star Is Born, A (1937), 180–81
Star Is Born, A (1954), 142–43, 184–85
Star Is Born, A (1976), 82–83, 94–95, 142–43
Star Trek: The Motion Picture (1979), 70–71
Star Wars (1977), 28–29, 66–67, 70–71, 72–73
Stay Away Joe (1968), 12–13
Steamboat Willie (1928), 114–15
Strange Love of Martha Ivers, The (1946), 174–75
Strangers on a Train (1951), 22–23, 180–81
Stratton Story, The (1949), 128–29
Streetcar Named Desire, A (1952), 10–11, 24–25
Summer of '42 (1971), 112–13
Summer Magic (1963), 114–15
Summertime (1955), 96–97
Sunset Boulevard (1950), 32–33, 74–75, 82–83, 140–41, 184–85
Superman (1978), 44–45, 106–07
Superman II (1981), 44–45
Sylvia (1965), 28–29
Sylvia Scarlett (1935), 46–47

Taming of the Shrew, The (1929), 158—59
Tarzan and His Mate (1934), 56–57
Tarzan, The Ape Man (1981), 182–83
Taxi Driver (1976), 52–53, 154–55, 184–85
Ten Commandments, The (1956), 22–23, 70–71, 154–55
Tess of the Storm Country (1922), 38–39
Texas Chainsaw Massacre, The (1974), 92–93
That Darned Cat! (1964), 26–27, 114–15
Them (1954), 114–15
There's No Business Like Show Business (1954), 126–27
These Three (1936), 56–57
They Died with Their Boots On (1941), 10–11
They Shoot Horses, Don't They? (1969), 184–85
They Were Expendable (1945), 84–85
Thing, The (1982), 64–65
39 Steps, The (1935), 124–25
This Gun For Hire (1942), 82–83
This Is the Army (1943), 62–63
Three Comrades (1938), 180–81
Three Days of the Condor (1975), 184–85
Three Godfathers (1948), 24–25
Tiger Makes Out, The (1967), 32–33
Tightrope (1984), 16–17
To Catch a Thief (1955), 172–73
To Have and Have Not (1945), 6–7, 26–27, 62–63
Tootsie (1983), 46–47, 184–85
Topper (1937), 142–43
Tortilla Flat (1942), 10–11
Treasure of the Sierra Madre, The (1947), 32–33, 48–49
Trog (1970), 110–11
Trouble with Harry, The (1955), 172–73, 174–75
Turning Point, The (1977), 40–41, 72–73
Twelve O'Clock High (1949), 48–49
Two-Faced Woman (1941), 194–95
Two Women (1961), 182–83

Ugly American, The (1962), 4–5
Uncle Tom's Cabin (1927), 20–21

Valentino (1977), 82–83
Valley of the Dolls (1967), 62–63
Vanishing Prairie, The (1954), 158–59
Vertigo (1958), 128–29
Victory Through Air Power (1943), 114–15
Viva Las Vegas (1964), 12–13
Viva Zapata (1952), 192–93

Watermelon Man (1970), 54–55
Way We Were, The (1973), 184–85
W. C. Fields and Me (1976), 140–41
Well-Groomed Bride, The (1946), 92–93
Whatever Happened to Baby Jane? (1962), 112–13
What's New, Pussycat? (1965), 90–91
What's Up, Tiger Lily? (1966), 8–9
When Worlds Collide (1951), 92–93
Where the Boys Are (1960), 12–13
White Heat (1949), 50–51
Who Is the Black Dahlia? (1975), 164–65
Who's Afraid of Virginia Woolf? (1966), 194–94, 198–99, 202–03
Wild Angels, The (1966), 92–93, 182–83
Wild Horse Mesa (1932), 166–67
Wild Ones, The (1954), 106–07
Willy Wonka and the Chocolate Factory (1971), 8–9
Winning (1969), 166–67
Winning of Barbara Worth, The (1926), 174–75
Wizard of Oz (1939), 84–85
Wolf Man, The (1941), 84–85
Woman of the Year (1942), 72–73
Won Ton Ton, the Dog Who Saved Hollywood (1976), 140–41
Woodstock (1970), 56–57
Wrong Man, The (1957), 180–81
Wuthering Heights (1939), 36–37, 42–43, 84–85

Yankee Doodle Dandy (1942), 184–85
Yearling, The (1946), 20–21
Year of Living Dangerously, The (1982), 46–47
You Can't Take It With You (1938), 108–09, 128–29
Young Man of Manhattan, The (1930), 90–91
You're in the Army Now (1940), 200–01

# BIOGRAPHICAL NOTES

Karen Warner and Michael Iapoce have worked together providing humorous material and pithy speeches for many of the country's top corporate executives.

Warner is also the founder of M.V.P., a firm that represents professional athletes who make public appearances. A trivia aficionado, she is co-author of *San Francisco Trivia*, which topped the Bay Area bestseller list shortly after its publication in 1985.

Iapoce has performed as a stand-up comic in many night clubs in the San Francisco Bay Area and written jokes for a number of nationally known comedians. Although he enjoys writing, he envies his brother-in-law, who is a film editor for MGM.